What others are saying about this book

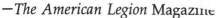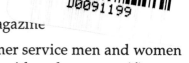

"Finding an old buddy ma[...]
the release of this book."
—*The American Legion* Magazine

"A book that can help former service men and women find friends they have served with or locate specific people to substantiate a claim."
—*Disabled American Veterans* Magazine

"The title of this specialized little niche-filler describes it perfectly. This book lists just about every conceivable private, federal, and state agency that one might contact."
—*American Reference Books Annual*

"The author has brought together a whole group of options available to those searching for military personnel."
—*The Genealogical Helper*

"I have accomplished more with this book in two months than I did in three years on my own. I have found all of my World War II unit."
—Howard Ashcraft, Virginia

"It will be valuable to users of public, some academic, and especially military libraries."
—*Booklist*, American Library Association

"This book is the standard in twentieth century military research."
—*Professional Genealogists' Quarterly*

Other favorable reviews and articles have been published by *VFW Magazine*, *AMVETS*, Air Force *Afterburner*, *Soldier of Fortune*, *International Combat Arms*, *The Retired Officer*, *Off Duty*, *Retired Military Family*, *Military Life*, *Semper Fidelis* as well as the *Philadelphia Inquirer* and *Stars and Stripes* newspaper. This book is listed in *Directories in Print*.

HOW TO LOCATE ANYONE WHO IS OR HAS BEEN IN THE MILITARY

Armed Forces Locator Guide

How to Locate Anyone Who Is or Has Been in the Military

Armed Forces Locator Guide

Lt. Col. Richard S. Johnson

7th Edition, Completely Revised

MIE Publishing

MIE Publishing
PO Box 17118
Spartanburg, SC 29301
(800) 937-2133
E-mail: miepublish@aol.com
http://www.eden.com/~mie

Library of Congress Cataloging in Publication Data:

Johnson, Richard S., 1933-

How to locate anyone who is or has been in the military:
Armed Forces locator guide
/Richard S. Johnson.—7th ed.
p. cm.

Includes index.
ISBN 1-877639-25-7

1. United States—Armed Forces—Registers.
2. Veterans—United States—Societies, etc.—Directories.
I. Title

U11.U5J54   1996
355'.0025'73—dc20   96-18890
                                              CIP

Dedication

This book is dedicated to the 27 million living veterans who have served their country with distinction.

Acknowledgements

It is impossible to cite all the authorities I have consulted in the preparation of this book; the list would include department heads in the Department of Defense, the Department of Veterans Affairs and other federal and state agencies.

I wish to acknowledge the contributions made by Charles Pellegrini of the National Personnel Records Center, Dick Bielen, Julie Delpho, and Debbie Knox for their assistance, Tom Ninkovich for editing and interior design, and George Foster for cover design. Special thanks to my wife, Mickey, for her sound advice.

Foreword

Lt. Col. Richard Johnson has provided a useful and welcomed service to all men and women who have been privileged to wear the military uniforms of our nation.

It is my opinion that virtually every veteran of our military services, in peace or war, does at some time want to contact a buddy with whom he or she served. Until now, that has been unusually difficult. But now, thanks to Colonel Johnson, it can be expeditiously accomplished.

—William C. Westmoreland
General, United States Army, Retired
Charleston, South Carolina

Table of Contents

HOW TO USE THIS BOOK

This book provides information on how to locate anyone who is or has been in the U.S. military. This includes active, retired, or former members of the Air Force, Army, Coast Guard, Marine Corps, Navy, the reserve and National Guard. There are many methods that can be used for finding these people, so it is recommended that you read the entire book before beginning your search.

The more information you have on an individual, the easier it will be to find him or her. Any of the following can be helpful in your search:

- Name (entire name or part)
- Service number
- Social Security number
- Date of birth
- Branch of service
- Current or former unit or ship assigned
- Base, post or city assigned
- Military job assigned
- Home of record
- Former address (military or civilian)

Most people are easy to locate. A few may take more time and effort. On difficult cases, you first might consider how badly you want to find the person. Difficult cases can take much time, effort and money.

We have added two new chapters in this edition—"Locating Women Veterans" and "Verifying Military Service." Additionally, there is a new chapter on case studies right at the beginning of the book so that the reader may better understand how others have used this information to locate people.

Chapters Two, Three and Four show how to locate anyone who is currently on active duty, is a member of the reserve and National Guard or is retired from any of these components. If you know the current status (active or retired) of the person, it is usually easy to find them.

Chapter Five deals with locating *veterans* of all branches of the armed forces and former members of the reserves and National Guard.

Veteran: A person who served on active duty in one or more of the armed forces.

Chapters Five, Six and Seven concern military reunions and veteran's organizations both of which can be helpful in locating a missing veteran.

Much information is provided in Chapters Eight and Twelve concerning military records, service numbers and Social Security numbers. Military records can contain important information such as units of assignment, date of birth, and place of entry into the military. All of this valuable identifying information can be used to provide a current address.

This book contains hundreds of telephone and fax numbers, area codes and addresses. Every attempt has been made to ensure that this information is current and correct. However, if you encounter a number that is incorrect, please call the area information operator, (area code) 555-1212 for the correct number. For toll free numbers, call (800) 555-1212. If you encounter a military telephone number that is incorrect, call the appropriate base information operator listed in the back of Chapter Two for the correct number. The Pentagon information operator, (703) 545-6700, can provide numbers for both the Washington DC area, and numbers for military installations worldwide. It is important to use the telephone wisely as it can save you time in your search.

Unfortunately, there is no database which equates service numbers to Social Security numbers. Refer to Chapter Twelve for additional information on service numbers and Social Security numbers.

After reading this book, it will be clear that there are many methods available to locate people who are or have been in the military. It may take more than one attempt to be successful, but if you are persistent you will ultimately find the person you are trying to locate.

If you have any questions concerning this book, please write to the author, Lt. Col. Richard S. Johnson, at the address below. We would also appreciate hearing about any successful searches. Since the information in this book changes at times, revised editions will be published annually. Any comments that may improve future copies of this book will certainly be appreciated. Many items have already been changed or added due to recommendations by readers. Write or fax us at the following address.

MIE Publishing
Lt. Col. Richard S. Johnson (Ret)
PO Box 340081
San Antonio, TX 78234
(210) 828-4667 Fax

Chapter 1

CASE STUDIES

The following case studies show how others have used the information in this book. Hopefully, they will give you an idea of how to apply this information to your particular situation.

Using the World-Wide Locator and Base Locator

David needed to talk to his son, Brad, who was in the Army. David did not know Brad's address and had not heard from him in over two years. David wrote to the Army World-Wide Locator (see Chapter Two) and asked for Brad's unit of assignment. Brad was in a unit at Fort Drum, New York. David called the base locator at Fort Drum which gave him Brad's work telephone number.

Using the World-Wide Locator

Joan wanted to find an old boyfriend who was on active duty in the Navy. She wrote to the Navy World-Wide Locator and gave them his name and

date of birth. They sent her the name and address of
the ship to which he was assigned.

Using the National Reunion Registry and VETS

Terry needed to find Cal Foster. He and Cal
served together in the Army in Vietnam. All he knew
was his buddy's name. First Terry called VETS (see
page 141) but they did not have any information
about a reunion group for his old unit. He then called
the National Reunion Registry (see page 142) and obtained the telephone number of a reunion group for
his unit. Cal was a member of this group. They gave
Terry Cal's address and telephone number. The two
have talked on the telephone and plan to get together soon.

Using the Department of Veterans Affairs

George desperately needed to find his old girl
friend whom he dated when they were both in the
Air Force. George knew that she had married, but
did not know her current last name. He knew her
date of birth so he called the VA. They were able to
identify her in their computer files and gave him her
new last name. He asked where her VA file was located. They responded that the file was at the VA Regional Office in Salt Lake City, Utah. He called
Directory Assistance in Utah and obtained her telephone number.

Using the Veterans Administration
and Computer Search

For over five years Ann had tried to find her
brother who had been in the Coast Guard. She did

not have his Social Security number but she had his date of birth. She wrote to the VA Records Processing Center and requested his VA Claim number. They returned the number which had nine digits and which was therefore also his SSN. With this she had a SSN Trace run (see Appendix B) and received his current address. She immediately contacted him. They are now planning a family reunion.

Using the National Personnel Records Center and the Department of Veterans Affairs

Randolph was born in England in 1955. His mother was English and his father was an American serviceman. He only knew that his father's name was John P. Smith and that he was in the U.S. Army stationed at a town near London. He wrote to the U.S. Military History Institute and obtained the units that were stationed near London in 1954–55. He then requested from the National Personnel Records Center the morning reports of these units for these years. He found his father's name and service number on one of the morning reports. He then contacted the VA who identified his father in their computer files. He sent a forwarded letter to him which was immediately answered.

Using a Historical Organization and Computer Search

Juanita never knew her natural father. She only knew his name and that he was stationed at an Army base near Baltimore in 1960. Her mother could not remember the exact spelling of her father's name but remembered that it was a common Latin Amer-

ican name. She contacted the U.S. Military History
Institute and obtained the unit designation. Next she
was able to obtain a unit yearbook of her father's unit
from a military historian. It had his picture and the
correct spelling of his complete legal name. There
were several listings for this exact name in the National Telephone Directory (see Appendix B). After a
few phone calls, she located her father. They have
met and visit each other frequently.

Using a Computer Search

Rosemary was adopted and wished to find her
natural mother who was a WAC in World War II.
From her original adoption papers she found her
mother's maiden name and date of birth. She had the
Nationwide Locator (see Appendix B) do a computer
DOB search. They entered the mother's first name
and DOB into the computer database. It returned the
first and last name of twenty-three people whose
first name and DOB matched. Her mother was located by telephone in three days. They will see each other in a few months when the shock wears off.

Using the National Personnel Records Center
and Computer Search

Wilbur wanted to locate his father. His parents
had divorced in 1950 when he was three. His father's
name was Darrell Schulz. His mother did not remember his father's DOB but she did have his service
number which was on the return address of a letter
he had sent her. Wilbur wrote to the National Personnel Records Center and requested his father's
records under the Freedom of Information Act. He

received the records which included his father's date of birth. He had the Nationwide Locator do a DOB computer search. They located his father in a few hours. Wilbur immediately contacted his father who had also been searching for Wilbur for years. They have met and have established a great relationship.

Using the National Personnel Records Center, VA, and Computer Searches

Joe was the reunion organizer for his ship which had served in Southeast Asia in 1966 and 1967. He wrote to the National Personnel Records Center and obtained copies of the ship muster rolls. These contained the names and service numbers of all the enlisted personnel who were assigned to the ship. He sent a copy of the names and service numbers to the VA Records Processing Center. This office had addresses on most of the men and dates of death on a few more. Joe located 60 percent of the crewmen through the VA. He located many others with computer searches and notices in veteran's magazines. Their first reunion will be this summer.

Using the American Medical Association

Hub needed to locate a doctor who had treated him in Panama. He needed information for a VA disability claim. Hub contacted the American Medical Association which provided him with the doctor's current address.

Using the Veterans Administration

Mary was chairman of her high school class reunion. She had located everyone except Thomas

Walker who went into the Army when he graduated in 1980. She knew Tom's date of birth so she called the VA who identified his file. She had a letter forwarded by the VA. Tom attended his class reunion.

Using the Social Security Administration

Ruth was adopted when she was a baby. When she became 21 she wanted find her birth mother. She obtained her adoption report from the agency that handled her adoption. The report listed her mother's name and date of birth. She called the Social Security Administration and asked if they could identify her mother in their computer files. They could, and also stated that they did not have a report of death on her. Ruth wrote a letter to her mother and sent it to the Social Security Administration which forwarded it to her mother. Ruth's mother responded immediately to her daughter.

Using the National Personnel Records Center

Ralph's mother told him his natural father was a serviceman whom she met at a dance. They dated for a few months, he was sent to Korea, and she never heard from him again. All she knew was his name, that he was a clerk and was assigned to an engineering unit stationed in Washington, DC. Ralph wrote to the Director of the National Personnel Records Center and included the information his mother had given him. A few months later the Center replied. They had identified his father from a unit roster and sent his father's legal name, service number and date of birth. They also provided Ralph with the name of the town where his father had lived when he separated from the Army. Ralph called Directory Assistance for that town. There was no listing for his father but there were two listings with the same last name. One was his father's brother who gave Ralph the address and telephone number of his father.

Using a Muster Roll, Personnel Records and Computer Search

Rebecca wished to find her mother's father whom her mother had never met. The only information they had was that his name was Fred Smith, he had been in the Navy, and had served on the USS Night Hawk in World War II. Rebecca contacted VETS and The National Reunion Registry to find out if the ship had a reunion organization. Neither had a reunion group listed. She then requested a muster roll of the ship from the National Archives. The muster roll listed her grandfather as Fred Q. Smith and showed his service number. Rebecca called the Department of Veterans Affairs. They had his name and service number in their computer file but no other information. Next she sent a request to the National Personnel Records Center under the Freedom of Information Act. They sent her a copy of his military records which listed his date of birth. Rebecca then requested a computer date of birth search. This provided his current address and telephone number. He lived in a city only an hour away from Rebecca.

Obtaining Records for a Family History

Debra had heard about the accomplishments of her grandfather who served in the Army during World Wars I and II. She had never seen anything about his service in writing so she decided to collect items for a family history. She obtained the normal items such as birth and death certificates, obituaries, school records, etc. She then wrote to the National Personnel Records Center and requested his complete military file (as next of kin). They sent a copy of his complete file. Next, she wrote to the Department of Veterans Affairs and requested his claims file. This was sent to her in a few weeks. Debra knew that her grandfather had also served in the National Guard in Texas between World Wars I and II. She wrote to the Adjutant General of Texas. This office sent his complete National Guard file in a few days. She also wrote to the State Archives and found that they had a copy of his mustering-in records from World War I. She also wrote to various historical organizations and was able to obtain a photo of him when he attended service school and a listing of him in an officer register. With this information Debra was able to prepare an excellent family history of her grandfather which she shared with other family members.

Locating a Female Veteran

Joan wished to locate Cindy whom she had served with in the Army during the Vietnam War. They had corresponded for several years after the war but lost contact about five years ago. She knew Cindy was planning on marrying another veteran but did not know his name. Joan's letters to the last address she had for Cindy were returned by the post office marked "moved—no forwarding address." Joan contacted several veteran organizations but they did not have any information. She contacted the Department of Veterans Affairs but they did could not identify her because Joan had only a name, branch of service and estimated date of birth. Joan had a computer "Retrace" done (see Appendix B) using Cindy's name and former address. This computer search uses the header information from credit files. The search provided her friend's current married name, current address and her Social Security number.

Verifying Military Service

Jack was an assistant professor at a small college in Mississippi. One of his colleagues claimed that he was in the Army and was on a "secret mission" that allowed him to teach at the college. This person often appeared at parties wearing an Army uniform with the insignia of a Major. He also had ribbons for several awards, including the Silver Star. Jack thought it was pretty strange for someone to be bragging that he was on a "secret mission." Several other things made Jack think that this person was an impostor. Jack obtained this person's date of birth from the college. With this information he wrote the Army World-Wide Locator. They told Jack that there was no record of that individual being in the Army. He reported his findings to the college which in turn asked the impostor for proof that he was in the Army. He could not provide proof. The college fired him immediately.

Verifying if a Person Is a Veteran

Hank was an officer in a veteran's organization. He was suspicious about Neil, another officer in the organization. Neil claimed that he had been wounded during the Korean War and had received the Purple Heart. To join this particular organization, each person was required to present a copy of his Report of Separation (DD 214). Hank examined Neil's DD 214. It appeared to have been altered. Hank wrote to the National Personnel Records Center and requested a copy of Neil's military records under the Freedom of Information Act. The records revealed that Neil had served in the military, but not during the Korean War nor had he received the Purple Heart. Hank presented this information to the organization's headquarters and Neil was expelled.

Chapter 2

LOCATING ACTIVE DUTY MILITARY

This chapter describes ways to locate members of the armed forces who are on active duty using:

- *The Armed Forces World-Wide Locators*
- *Base and Post Locators*
- *Army, Air Force and Fleet Post Offices (APOs and FPOs)*

Armed Forces World-Wide Locators

The Armed Forces World-Wide Locators will either forward a letter or provide current military unit of assignment. The latter may be limited to unit of assignment in the United States.

If you wish to have a letter forwarded, place the letter in a sealed, stamped envelope. Put your name and return address in the upper left-hand corner. In the center of the envelope put the rank, full name of the person sought, followed by the Social Security number or date of birth (if known). On a separate sheet of paper put everything you know that may help the military locator such as:

- Name
- Rank
- Social security number
- Military service, e.g., active Air Force
- Date of birth (estimated, if actual is unknown)
- Sex
- Officer or enlisted (if rank is not available)
- Date entered service
- Last assignment (if known)

In another envelope, preferably legal size, enclose the letter you want forwarded along with the fact sheet and a check for the search fee. (The current search fee for all armed forces is $3.50. Make check payable to Treasurer of the U.S.) If *you* are active, reserve, National Guard, retired military or a family member, state this on the fact sheet. Show your rank and SSN or relationship, and the search fee will be waived. On the outer envelope include your name and return address. Address it to the appropriate locator below.

If the military locator can identify the individual, your letter will be forwarded. It is up to the individual to reply to your letter. The military cannot require a reply through this process. If the military locator cannot identify the person you are seeking, it will return your letter and tell you why. Common problems include: the locator cannot identify the individual without a SSN (often the name is too common); the individual separated from the service; the SSN is incorrect; or the individual is deceased.

To determine to what unit and military installation a person is assigned, write a letter to the appropriate address below and include as much information as possible that will assist in identifying the person (include the same information as shown above).

If you already know the installation, you can call directly to that installation's assistance operator or the installation locator (see instructions under "Base and Post Locator Service" in this chapter). You can also mail a letter to the individual in care of the installation locator (see list of Base and Post locators for proper mailing address).

Locating Active Duty Air Force Personnel

The Air Force Locator will forward only one letter per each request and will not provide overseas unit of assignment of active members. Requests with more than one address per letter will be returned without action. Include a self-addressed stamped envelope with request for unit assignment. If the individual is separated from the Air Force, you will be informed.

U.S. Air Force World-Wide Locator
AFPC-MSIMDL
550 C. Street West, Suite 50
Randolph AFB, TX 78150-4752
(210) 652-5775, (210) 652-5774 Recording
http://www.afpc.af.mil
($3.50 fee)

The Air Force Locator has base assignment information on Air Force personnel since 1971. Include former base assignments with your request.

Locating Active Duty Army Personnel

The Army Locator furnishes military addresses for individuals currently serving on active duty in the Army and for the Department of the Army civilians. All requests must contain the individual's full name and the Social Security number or date of birth. No information will be given without one of the above identifying numbers. Their hours of operation are 7:30 a.m. to 4:00 p.m. EST, Monday through Friday. Written requests should be mailed to the above address with a check or money order in the amount of $3.50 for each name submitted. Check or money order should be made payable to "Finance Officer" (do not send cash). Approximate time for processing written requests is seven to ten working days.

The locator system holds separation data for two years after a soldier is separated. The only separation data available is date and place of separation.

To forward a letter to an active duty member, put your return address on the envelope to be forwarded and in the body of the letter of request.

World-Wide Locator
U.S. Army Enlisted Records
    and Evaluation Center
8899 East 56th Street
Indianapolis, IN 46249-5301
(703) 325-3732
http://www.army.mil/vetinfo/persloc.htm

For bona fide emergencies, call Total Army Personnel Command Staff Duty Officer at (703) 325-8851. This office has the microfiche of all individuals currently on active duty in the Army and all retired Army personnel. It is open 24 hours a day. Also refer to the American Red Cross (see page 22).

Locating Active Duty Coast Guard Personnel

The Coast Guard will provide ship or station of assignment and unit telephone number of active duty personnel when requested by telephone. A $5.20 search fee is charged for a *written* verification of unit assignment. If you know the ship to which the member is assigned, consult the Fleet Post Office listing in this chapter.

> Commandant
> (CGPC-ADM-3)
> U.S. Coast Guard
> 2100 Second Street, S.W.
> Washington, DC 20593-0001
> (202) 267-1340, (202) 267-4985 Fax
> ($3.50 fee)

Locating Active Duty Marine Corps Personnel

> U.S. Marine Corps-CMC
> (MMSB-10)
> 2008 Elliot Road, Room 201
> Quantico, VA 22134-5030
> (703) 784-3942
> ($3.50 fee)

Locating Active Duty Navy Personnel

> Bureau of Naval Personnel
> PERS-324
> 2 Navy Annex
> Washington, DC 20370-3240

(703) 614-5011, (703) 614-3155 Recording

(703) 614-1261 Fax

http://www.navy.mil/navpalib/people/faq/.ww
w/locate.html

($3.50 fee)

The previous locator will only forward letters. If you know the name of the ship to which the member is assigned, see Fleet Post Office listing in this chapter.

Base and Post Locator Service

The armed forces provide locator services at most of their installations. The Freedom of Information Act provides that the services may release a military member's unit or ship assignment. They may also provide their duty telephone number. You may need to provide SSN or rank if there is more than one person with the same name. You can call the locator if you know the installation where the person is assigned. Locators normally operate from 7:00 or 7:30 a.m. to 4:00 or 4:30 p.m., Monday through Friday. The locator service usually has its own office at larger bases. However, sometimes the service is provided by the telephone information operator, the personnel office or by the Staff Duty Officer (SDO) after normal working hours and holidays. When you call, give the name and rank of the person you are looking for and ask for their duty assignment, work telephone number, home address and telephone number. Some individuals may have authorized release of their home addresses and telephone numbers.

Many enlisted people live in barracks, dormitories or quarters on the base as do many single non-commissioned officers (NCOs) and officers. These can be contacted through the Charge of Quarters of their unit after normal duty hours. Some married NCOs and officers live on base in quarters and have telephone numbers that are available through the local telephone company. Call the local civilian information operator to find out if they have a listed telephone number. Many military members live in the civilian communities close to the military installation to which they are assigned.

To obtain the telephone number of an installation locator not listed in the following pages, call the installation information operator to get the number. If you know the unit of the person you are trying to reach, the operator can give you that telephone number. You may also write to the locator to obtain the number. The Base or Post Locator keeps forwarding addresses for personnel who are separated from the service or personnel who have been transferred for six months after departure. Mail for personnel who were assigned to decommissioned ships or closed installations will be forwarded for sixty days after closing or decommissioning.

Armed Forces Installations

A list of U.S. Military Installations is available at the end of this chapter. This information may be used to locate current military members assigned to a particular installation by either calling or writing the Base or Post Locator. Telephone numbers of units, offices and individuals who live in base quarters may be obtained through the base and post information operator.

Child Support—Collecting from Active Duty Military

To obtain the current address of active duty military for child support collection, contact your local county or city child support enforcement agency (listed in your local telephone directory). The agency can then contact the appropriate armed forces World-Wide Locator listed in this chapter to obtain the military member's current assignment. All submissions must be made in writing on the agency letterhead. There are no fees charged for this service. List as much information as is known about the person, such as: complete legal name; social security number; date of birth; rank; and last place of assignment.

The same process should be done for locating a retired military member for child support collection. See Chapter Four for a list of addresses to locate retired military.

American Red Cross

The American Red Cross, under federal statute, and in accordance with regulations of the armed forces, has one or more representatives at each military installation to deal with families of military members concerning family emergencies.

To locate a member of the armed forces (who is on active duty or active duty for training) because of an emergency in their family, such as a death or serious illness, do not contact the military, but call your local Red Cross chapter. They are listed in the telephone book. Tell the Red Cross representative the nature of the emergency and the name, rank, and service of the military member. The Red Cross will immediately verify the matter and forward a message via Red Cross channels to the military member. Upon request of the member, the verified information will be passed to the military authorities to assist them to make a decision regarding emergency leave. Both the Red Cross and military have guidelines under which they work. While it is not necessary for the military to have a Red Cross verification in order to grant leave in emergency situations, they normally request it. The American Red Cross is the best way to contact a military member when there is a crisis at home. For more information regarding Red Cross services contact your local Red Cross office. The following address is for the national office of the American Red Cross emergency services department.

American Red Cross/Emergency Services
8111 Gatehouse Road
Falls Church, VA 22042
(703) 206-7550, (703) 206-7430

Locating Military Personnel through Banks, Credit Unions and Insurance Companies

As a service to their members and customers many banks, credit unions and insurance companies (automobile, life and home owners) will forward letters to their customers. If you know a financial institution of the person you are looking for, this can be an excellent way to locate them. Before you attempt this, you should contact the institution first to ensure that they will forward your letter. Some of these institutions provide this service for their members and customers only. There are several large national insurance companies and associations that do all or most of their business with members of the armed forces. Many of their customers continue this business relationship after they separate or retire from the military.

Base information telephone operators can normally give you the name and number of banks and credit unions that have offices on their base. See Base and Post Locator Directory in this chapter for the appropriate telephone numbers.

Obtain Unit Address of Active Duty Military by Computer or Telephone

CSRA, Inc., provides information on active duty military quickly by computer or telephone. Request a search by telephone directly from CSRA or on-line using a computer. The following information is available:

- Name
- Pay grade
- Unit of assignment
- Base and zip code
- Military job code
- Date of entry
- Date of termination of service agreement

For further information and prices contact:

CSRA, Inc.
23 Rock Knoll
Irvine, CA 92715
(800) 327-2720, (714) 509-9119 Fax

Armed Forces Installations in the United States

The following pages list the major military installations in the Unites States and its territories. It gives the name of the installation, the zip code, the base/post information number and the base locator number. Many installations have the information and locator at the same number.

This information may be used to locate current military members assigned to a particular installation by either calling or writing the base or post locator. To address a letter to a specific base the first line should be: "Attention: Base Locator."

Telephone numbers of units, offices and individuals who live in base quarters may be obtained through the base and post information operator.

The following abbreviations are used in this list:

AAF	–	Army Air Field
AF	–	Air Force
AFB	–	Air Force Base
AFRB	–	Air Force Reserve Base
AFS	–	Air Force Station
AMC	–	Army Medical Center
ANG	–	Air National Guard
CG	–	Coast Guard
CGAS	–	Coast Guard Air Station
HQ	–	Headquarters
MC	–	Marine Corps
MCAS	–	Marine Corps Air Station
NAB	–	Naval Amphibious Base
NAS	–	Naval Air Station
NS	–	Naval Station
NSA	–	Naval Support Activity
NSB	–	Naval Submarine Base Station
NWS	–	Naval Weapons Station

ALABAMA:

Anniston Army Depot	36201	(205) 235-7501	235-7501
Dannelly Field ANG	36125	(334) 284-7100	284-7411
Fort McClellan	36205	(205) 848-4611	848-3281
Fort Rucker	36362	(334) 255-1030	255-3156
Gunter Annex	36114	(334) 416-1110	953-5027
Maxwell AFB	36114	(334) 416-1110	953-5027
MobileCoast Guard Aviation Training Center	36608	(334) 639-6101	639-6125
MobileCoast Guard Base	36608	(334) 639-6125	639-6125
Redstone Arsenal	35898	(205) 876-2151	876-3331

ALASKA:

Adak Naval Air Facility	99506	(907) 592-4201	592-4201
Attu Coast Guard Station	99615	(907) 392-3315	392-3315
Clear Air Force Station	99704	(907) 585-6113	585-6209
Eilson Air Force Base	99702	(907) 377-1110	377-1841
Elmendorf AFB	99506	(907) 552-1110	552-4860
Fort Greely	99508	(907) 873-1121	873-3255
Fort Richardson	99505	(907) 384-1110	384-0306
Fort Wainwright	99703	(907) 353-1110	353-6898
Integrated Support Command Ketchikan	99901	(907) 228-0212	228-0212
King Salmon Airport	99613	(907) 552-1110	552-4860
Kodiak CG Air Station	99619	(907) 487-5163	487-5163
Kodiak CG Support Ctr	99619	(907) 487-5170	487-5170
Kulis ANG Base	99502	(907) 249-1239	249-1239
Sitka CG Air Station	99835	(907) 966-5556	966-5556

ARIZONA:

Arizona ANG	85034	(602) 302-9000	302-9000
Davis-Monthan AFB	85707	(520) 750-3900	750-3347
Fort Huachuca	85613	(520) 538-7111	538-7111
Gila Bend AF Auxiliary Fld	85337	(520) 683-6261	683-6261
Luke AFB	85309	(602) 856-7411	856-6405
Yuma MC Air Station	85369	(520) 341-2011	341-2011
Yuma Proving Ground	85365	(602) 328-3287	328-3287

ARKANSAS:

Fort Chaffee	72905	(501) 484-2141	484-2933
Little Rock AFB	72099	(501) 988-3131	988-6025
Pine Bluff Arsenal	71602	(501) 540-3000	540-3000

CALIFORNIA:

Alameda CG Support Center	94501	(510) 437-2904	437-2904
Alameda NAS	94501	(510) 263-3012	263-3012
Barstow MC Logistical Base	92311	(619) 577-6211	577-6675
Bridgeport Marine Corps Mtn. Warfare Center	92155	(619) 932-7761	932-7761
Beale AFB	95903	(916) 634-3000	634-2960
CGAS Humboldt Bay	95521	(707) 839-6103	839-6103
Camp Pendleton	92055	(619) 725-4111	725-4111
Camp Roberts	93451	(805) 238-3100	238-3100
Camp San Luis Obispo	93403	(805) 594-6201	594-6201
China Lake Naval Air Weapons Station	93555	(619) 437-2011	939-9011
Concord Naval Weapons Stn	94520	(510) 246-2000	246-5040
Coronado NAB	92155	(619) 437-2011	437-2011
Costa Mesa ANG Station	92627	(714) 668-2300	668-2323
Edwards AFB	93523	(805) 277-1110	277-2777
El Centro Naval Air Facility	92243	(619) 437-2011	339-2524
El Toro MC Air Station	92709	(714) 726-2100	726-3736
Fort Hunter Liggett	93928	(408) 386-3000	386-3000
Fort Irwin	92310	(619) 380-1111	380-1111
Fresno ANG Base	93727	(209) 454-5100	454-5100
Hayward ANG Station	94545	(510) 783-1661	783-1661
Imperial Beach NS	91933	(619) 437-2011	437-2011
Lemoore Naval Air Station	93246	(209) 998-0100	998-3789
Long Beach Naval Shipyard	90822	(310) 547-6721	547-6004
Los Angeles AFB	90245	(310) 363-1000	363-1876
Los Angeles CGAS	90045	(310) 215-2204	215-2204
March AFB	92518	(909) 655-1110	655-1110
McClellan AFB	95652	(916) 643-2111	643-2111
Miramar Naval Station	92145	(619) 437-2011	537-6018
Monterey CG Group	93940	(408) 647-7300	647-7300
Monterey Naval Postgraduate School	93943	(408) 656-2441	656-2441
North Island Naval Station	92135	(619) 437-2011	545-9178
Oakland Army Base	94626	(510) 466-9111	466-2509
Oakland Naval Medical Ctr	94627	(510) 633-5000	633-5000
Oakland Naval Supply Ctr	94625	(510) 302-2000	302-2000
Onizuka Air Station	94089	(408) 752-3000	752-4539
Petaluma CG Training Ctr	94952	(770) 765-7211	765-7211
Point Reyes CG Station	94956	(415) 669-2000	669-2003
Port Hueneme ANG Stn	93041	(805) 986-8000	986-8000

Port Hueneme Naval Construction Battalion Ctr	93043	(805) 982-4711	982-5333
Presidio of Monterey	93944	(408) 242-5000	647-5119
Sacramento CGAS	95652	(916) 643-2081	643-2081
San Diego CGAS	92101	(619) 683-6330	683-6330
San Diego MC Recruit Depot	92140	(619) 437-2011	524-1719
San Diego Naval Medical Ctr	92134	(619) 437-2011	532-6400
San Diego Naval Station	92136	(619) 437-2011	556-1011
San Diego NSB	92106	(619) 437-2011	553-8663
San Diego Naval Training Ctr	92133	(619) 437-2011	524-1935
San Francisco CGAS	94128	(415) 876-2920	876-2920
Santa Clara Naval Air Reserve	94035	(415) 603-9527	603-9527
Seal Beach Naval Weapons	90740	(310) 626-7011	626-7692
Sharpe Army Depot	95331	(209) 982-2000	982-2003
Sierra Army Depot	96113	(916) 827-4000	827-4328
Tracy Defense Depot	95296	(209) 982-2000	982-2003
Travis AFB	94535	(707) 424-1110	424-2798
Treasure Island NS	94130	(415) 395-1000	395-3491
Twentynine Palms Air- Ground Combat Center	92278	(619) 830-6000	830-6000
Vandenberg AFB	93437	(805) 734-8232	734-8232

COLORADO:

Buckley ANG Base	80011	(303) 340-9011	340-9011
Denver Air Force Reserve Personnel Center	80279	(303) 676-6307	676-6307
Falcon AFB	80912	(719) 567-1110	567-5305
Fitzsimons AMC	80045	(303) 361-8241	361-8802
Fort Carson	80913	(719) 526-5811	526-0227
Peterson AFB	80914	(719) 556-7321	556-4020
Pueblo Army Depot	81001	(719) 549-4111	549-4111
Rocky Mountain Arsenal	80022	(303) 288-0711	288-0711
U.S. Air Force Academy	80840	(719) 472-1818	472-4262

CONNECTICUT:

Bradley ANG Base	06026	(203) 623-8291	623-8291
Long Island Sands CG Base	06512	(203) 468-4450	468-4450
New London NSB	06349	(860) 449-4636	449-3087
Orange Air Nat'l Guard Communications Station	06477	(203) 795-4786	795-4786
U.S. Coast Guard Academy	06320	(860) 444-8444	444-8444

DELAWARE:

Dover AFB	19902	(302) 677-2113	677-3000

DISTRICT OF COLUMBIA:

Andrews AFB	20762	(301) 981-1110	981-1110
Bolling AFB	20332	(703) 545-6700	767-4522*
Coast Guard HQ	20593	(202) 366-4000	366-4000
District of Columbia ANG	20762	(301) 981-1110	836-8257
Fort McNair	20319	(703) 545-6700	475-2005*
Marine Barracks	20390	(703) 545-6700	433-3793*
Marine Corps HQ	20380	(703) 614-2479	614-1235
Naval Security Station	20393	(202) 764-0211	764-0211
Navy Yard	20374	(202) 889-4909	433-3273*
Pentagon	20310	(703) 545-6700	545-6700
Walter Reed AMC	20307	(202) 782-3501	782-1150
Washington Naval Air Facility	20390	(301) 981-5848	433-3273*
National Guard Bureau	20310	(703) 697-4841	697-4841

*Area code (202)

FLORIDA:

Avon Park Air Force Range	33825	(947) 452-4114	452-4114
Camp Blanding	32091	(904) 533-3100	533-3100
Cape Canaveral AFS	32925	(407) 853-1110	494-4542
Cecil Field NAS	32215	(904) 778-5626	778-5240
Clearwater CG Air Station	34622	(813) 535-1437	535-1437
Corry Naval Station	32511	(904) 452-2000	452-6226
Duke Field AFS	32542	(904) 882-1110	882-1110
Eglin AFB	32542	(904) 882-1110	882-1110
Homestead AF Reserve Base	33039	(305) 224-7000	224-7138
Hurlburt Field	32544	(904) 882-1110	882-1110
Jacksonville NAS	32212	(904) 772-2338	772-2340
Cecil Field Naval Air Station	32215	(904) 778-5626	778-5240
Key West Coast Guard Group	33040	(305) 292-9735	292-9735
Key West Naval Air Station	33040	(305) 293-2268	293-2268
MacDill AFB	33621	(813) 828-1110	828-2444
Mayport Coast Guard Base	32267	(904) 247-7301	247-7301
Mayport Naval Station	32228	(904) 270-5011	270-5407
Miami CGAS	33054	(305) 953-2100	953-2100
Miami Coast Guard Base	33139	(305) 535-4300	535-4300
Miami Seventh CG District	33131	(305) 536-6990	536-6990
Orlando Naval Training Ctr	32813	(407) 646-4111	646-4501

Panama City Naval Coastal			
System Center	32407	(904) 234-4011	234-4011
Patrick AFB	32925	(407) 494-1110	494-1110
Pensacola Naval Air Technical			
Training Center	32508	(904) 452-0111	452-4693
Pensacola Naval Hospital	32512	(904) 452-6601	452-1519
Saufley Field	32509	(904) 452-1300	452-4519
Tyndall AFB	32403	(904) 283-1113	283-1113
Whiting Field NAS	32570	(904) 623-7011	623-7437

GEORGIA:

Albany MC Logistics Base	31704	(912)-439-5000	439-5103
Athens Naval Supply Corps			
School	30606	(706) 354-1500	354-1500
Atlanta Naval Air Station	30060	(770) 919-5000	919-5000
Camp Merrill	30533	(706) 864-3367	864-3367
Dobbins AFB	30069	(770) 919-5000	919-5000
Fort Benning	31905	(706) 545-2011	545-5217
Fort Gillem	30050	(404) 363-5000	752-3113
Fort Gordon	30905	(706) 791-0110	791-4675
Fort McPherson	30330	(404) 752-3113	752-3113
Fort Stewart	31314	(912) 767-1110	767-2862
Hunter Army Airfield	31409	(912) 767-1110	767-2862
Kings Bay NSB	31547	(912) 673-2001	673-2160
Moody AFB	31699	(912) 257-4211	257-3585
Robins AFB	31098	(912) 926-1110	926-1110
Savannah CG Air Station	31409	(912) 352-6237	352-6237

HAWAII:

Army Recreation Ctr	96792	(808) 471-7110	655-2299
Barbers Point CGAS	96862	(808) 682-2621	682-2621
Barbers Point NAS	96862	(808) 471-7110	684-1005
Barking Sands Pacific			
Missile Range/USN	96752	(808) 471-7110	614-3155
Bellows AFS	96853	(808) 471-7110	449-0165
Camp Smith, MC	96861	(808) 471-7110	477-0411
Eastern Pacific Naval Computer			
Telecommunications Stn	96786	(808) 471-7110	614-3155
Fort Shafter	96858	(808) 471-7110	655-2299
Helemano Military Reservtn	96857	(808) 471-7110	655-2299
Hickam AFB	96853	(808) 471-7110	449-0165
Kaneohe Bay MC Base	96863	(808) 471-7110	257-1294

Kunia Field Station	96819	(808) 471-7110	655-2299
Lualualei Naval Magazine	96792	(808) 471-7110	614-3155
Naval Ammo Area	96786	(808) 471-7110	614-3155
Pearl Harbor Naval Base	96860	(808) 471-7110	614-3155
Pohakuloa Training Area	96720	(808) 471-7110	614-3155
Sand Island CG Base	96819	(808) 541-2481	541-2481
Schofield Barracks	96857	(808) 471-7110	655-2299
Tripler Army Medical Ctr	96859	(808) 471-7110	433-6661
Wheeler Army Air Field	96854	(808) 471-7110	655-2299

IDAHO:

Gowen ANG Base	83705	(208) 422-5011	422-5011
Mountain Home AFB	83648	(208) 828-1110	828-6647

ILLINOIS:

Chicago CG Air Station	60026	(708) 657-2145	657-2145
Great Lakes Naval Trng Ctr	60088	(708) 688-3500	688-3500
O'Hare Air Reserve Facility	60666	(312) 825-6000	825-6000
Price Support Center	62040	(618) 452-4212	452-4212
Rock Island Arsenal	61299	(309) 782-6001	782-6001
Scott AFB	62225	(618) 256-1110	256-1841

INDIANA:

Camp Atterbury	46124	(812) 526-9711	526-9711
Crane Naval Weapons Support Center	47522	(812) 854-2511	854-2511
Fort Benjamin Harrison	46249	(317) 546-9211	542-4537
Grissom Reserve Center	46971	(317) 688-5211	688-5211
Indiana ANG HQ	47803	(812) 877-5210	877-5210
Indianapolis Naval Air Warfare Center	46219	(317) 359-8471	353-7339
Jefferson Proving Ground	47250	(812) 273-2511	273-2511

IOWA:

Des Moines ANG Base	50321	(515) 256-8210	256-8210

KANSAS:

9th MC District	66204	(816) 843-3882	843-3882
Forbes Field ANG Base	66619	(913) 862-1234	862-1234
Fort Leavenworth	66027	(913) 684-4021	684-3651
Fort Riley	66442	(913) 239-3911	239-9868

McConnell AFB	67221	(316) 652-6100	652-3555

KENTUCKY:

Fort Campbell	42223	(502) 798-2151	798-7196
Fort Knox	40121	(502) 624-1000	624-1141
Louisville Naval Ordinance Station	40214	(502) 364-5011	364-5011
Standford Field ANG Base	40213	(502) 364-9400	364-9400

LOUISIANA:

Barksdale AFB	71110	(318) 456-2252	456-3555
Camp Beauregard	71360	(318) 640-2080	640-2080
Fort Polk	71459	(318) 531-2911	531-1272
Navy Reserve Personnel Ctr	70149	(504) 678-6738	678-6738
New Orleans Coast Guard Support Center	70146	(504) 271-6262	271-6262
New Orleans Joint Reserve	70143	(504) 678-3253	678-3253
New Orleans NSA	70142	(504) 678-5011	361-2762

MAINE:

Bangor ANG	04401	(207) 990-7700	990-7700
Brunswick Naval Air Station	04011	(207) 921-2214	921-2214
Camp Keyes	04333	(207) 622-9331	622-9331
Naval Computer & Telecommunications Stn	04630	(207) 259-8229	259-8229
South Portland ANG Station	04106	(207) 767-1721	767-1721
South Portland CG Base	04106	(207) 767-0320	767-0333
Southwest Harbor CG Base	04679	(207) 244-5517	244-5517
Winter Harbor Naval Security Group	04693	(207) 963-5534	963-5534

MARYLAND:

Aberdeen Proving Ground	21005	(410) 278-5201	278-5138
Andrews AFB	20331	(301) 981-1110	981-1110
Annapolis Naval Station	21402	(410) 293-3972	293-3972
Army Research Laboratories	20783	(301) 394-2515	394-2515
Bethesda Naval Medical Ctr	20889	(301) 295-4611	295-4611
Curtis Bay Coast Guard Yard	21226	(410) 789-1600	789-1600
Edgewood Arsenal	21010	(410) 278-5201	278-5138
Fort Detrick	21702	(301) 619-8000	619-2233
Fort Meade	20755	(301) 677-6261	677-6261
Fort Ritchie	21719	(301) 878-1300	878-5685

Indian Head Naval Ordinance Station	20640	(301) 743-4000	743-4000
Patuxent River NAS	20670	(301) 342-3000	342-3000
Solomons Navy Rec Center	20688	(410) 326-4216	326-4216
U.S. Naval Academy	21402	(410) 293-1000	293-1000

MASSACHUSETTS:

Boston CG Support Center	02109	(617) 223-3257	223-3257
Camp Edwards	02542	(508) 968-1000	968-1000
Cape Cod CGAS	02548	(508) 968-1000	968-1000
Hanscom AFB	01731	(617) 377-4441	377-5111
Natick Army R&D Eng Ctr	01760	(508) 233-4000	233-4001
Otis ANG Base	02542	(508) 968-1000	968-1000
South Weymouth NAS	02190	(617) 682-2500	682-2933
Westover AFB	01022	(413) 557-1110	557-3874
Worcester ANGB Base	01605	(508) 799-6963	799-6963

MICHIGAN:

Camp Grayling	49739	(517) 348-7621	348-7621
Collins ANG Base	49707	(517) 354-6550	354-6550
Detroit CGAS	48045	(810) 307-6700	307-6700
Detroit Coast Guard Base	48207	(313) 568-9483	568-9483
Detroit Coast Guard Group	48207	(313) 568-9525	568-9525
Detroit Naval Air Reserve	48045	(810) 307-4011	307-4021
Grand Haven Coast Guard	49417	(616) 847-4500	847-4517
Selfridge ANG Base	48045	(810) 307-4011	307-4021
S. St. Marie CG Base	49783	(906) 635-3217	635-3217
Traverse City CG Air Station	49684	(616) 922-8214	922-8214

MINNESOTA:

Camp Ripley	56345	(612) 632-6631	632-6631
Twin City AF Reserve Base	55417	(612) 725-5011	725-5011

MISSISSIPPI:

Columbus AFB	39710	(601) 434-7322	434-7298
Gulfport Naval Construction Battalion Center	39501	(601) 871-2555	871-2555
Keesler AFB	39534	(601) 377-1110	377-2798
Meridian Naval Air Station	39309	(601) 679-2211	679-2528
Mississippi ANG HQ	39202	(601) 973-6123	973-6123
Naval Oceanography	39529	(601) 688-2211	688-2211
Thompson Field	39208	(601) 939-3633	939-3633

MISSOURI:

Army AG Publications Ctr	63114	(314) 263-3901	263-7722
Army Reserve Personnel Ctr	63132	(314) 263-3566	263-3566
Fort Leonard Wood	65473	(314) 596-0131	596-0677
Marine Corps Finance Ctr	64197	(816) 926-7652	926-7652
Saint Louis Coast Guard HQ	63103	(314) 539-7054	539-2662
Whiteman AFB	65305	(816) 687-1110	687-1841

MONTANA:

Malmstrom AFB	59402	(406) 731-1110	731-4121

NEBRASKA:

Nebraska ANG HQ	68524	(402) 471-3241	471-3241
Offutt AFB	68113	(402) 294-1110	294-5125

NEVADA:

Fallon Naval Air Station	89496	(702) 426-5161	426-2709
Indian Sprgs Air Force Auxiliary Field	89018	(702) 652-1110	652-8134
Nellis AFB	89191	(702) 652-1110	652-8134

NEW HAMPSHIRE:

Pease ANG Base	03803	(603) 430-3560	430-3560
Portsmouth Naval Shipyard	03804	(207) 438-1000	438-1555

NEW JERSEY:

Cape May CG Training Ctr	08204	(609) 898-6900	898-6900
Fort Dix	08640	(609) 562-1011	562-6051
Fort Monmouth	07703	(908) 532-9000	532-9000
Lakehurst Naval Air Engineering Station	08733	(908) 323-2011	323-2011
McGuire AFB	08641	(609) 724-1100	724-1100
Military Ocean Terminal Command	07002	(201) 823-5111	823-5111
Picatinny Arsenal	07806	(201) 724-4021	724-4021
Trenton Naval Warfare Ctr	08628	(609) 538-6600	538-6600

NEW MEXICO:

Cannon AFB	88103	(505) 784-3311	784-3311
Holloman AFB	88330	(505) 475-6511	475-7510
Kirtland AFB	87117	(505) 846-0011	846-0011
White Sands Missile Range	88002	(505) 678-2121	678-2121

NEW YORK:

Brooklyn CG Air Station	11234	(718) 615-2410	615-2421
Buffalo Coast Guard Group	14203	(716) 843-9504	843-9504
Fort Drum	13602	(315) 772-6900	772-5869
Fort Hamilton	11252	(718) 630-4101	630-4101
Fort Totten	11359	(718) 352-5700	352-5635
Governors Island CG Base	10004	(212) 668-7789	668-7739
Griffiss AFB	13441	(315) 330-1110	330-1110
New York ANG HQ	12110	(518) 786-4502	786-4502
Niagara Falls AF Reserve Base	14304	(716) 236-2000	236-2000
Roslyn ANG Station	11576	(516) 299-5229	299-5215
Seneca Army Depot	14541	(607) 869-1110	869-1110
Soctia Naval Administration	12302	(518) 395-3600	395-3600
Stewart ANG Base	12550	(914) 563-2000	563-2000
Stewart Army Subpost	12550	(914) 938-4011	938-4011
U.S. Army Military Academy	10996	(914) 938-4011	938-4011
Watervliet Arsenal	12189	(518) 266-5111	266-5111

NORTH CAROLINA:

Badin ANG Station	28009	(704) 422-2461	422-2461
Camp Lejeune MC Base	28542	(910) 451-1113	451-3074
Cape Hatteras CG Group	27920	(919) 995-6652	995-6652
Cherry Point MC Air Station	28533	(919) 466-2811	466-2811
Elizabeth City CG Air Station	27909	(919) 335-6000	338-3941
Fort Bragg	28307	(910) 396-0011	396-1461
Fort Macon CG Base	28512	(919) 247-4598	247-4598
New River MCAS	28545	(910) 451-1113	451-6508
Pope AFB	28308	(910) 394-0001	394-4822
Seymour Johnson AFB	27531	(919) 736-5400	736-5584
Sunny Point Military Ocean Terminal	28461	(910) 457-8000	457-8000

NORTH DAKOTA:

Cavalier AFS	58220	(701) 993-3297	993-3296
Grand Forks AFB	58205	(701) 747-3000	747-3344
North Dakota ANG HQ	58102	(701) 237-6030	237-6030
Minot AFB	58705	(701) 723-1110	723-1841

OHIO:

Blue Ash ANG Station	45242	(513) 792-2840	792-2840
Coast Guard Marine Safety Office	44114	(216) 522-4405	522-4405

Dayton Defense Electronics			
Supply Center	45420	(513) 296-5111	296-5111
Defense Construction			
Supply Center	43216	(614) 692-3131	692-4165
Navy Finance Center	44199	(216) 522-5630	522-5630
Newark Air Force Station	43057	(614) 522-2171	522-2171
Perry ANG Station	43452	(419) 635-4021	635-4021
Rickenbacker ANG Base	43217	(614) 492-4595	492-4595
Wright-Patterson AFB	45433	(513) 257-1110	257-3231

OKLAHOMA:

Altus AFB	73523	(405) 482-8100	481-7250
Army Ammo Plant	74501	(918) 421-2524	421-2524
Camp Gruber	74423	(918) 487-6001	487-6041
Fort Sill	73503	(405) 442-8111	442-3924
Oklahoma City ANG Base	73159	(405) 686-5210	736-7711
Tinker AFB	73145	(405) 732-7321	732-7321
Tulsa ANG	74115	(918) 832-8300	832-8300
Vance AFB	73705	(405) 237-2121	249-7791

OREGON:

Camp Rilea	97146	(503) 861-4000	861-4000
Kingsley Field ANG Base	97603	(541) 885-6350	885-6350
North Bend CGA Station	97459	(541) 756-9258	756-9220
Umatilla Army Depot	97838	(541) 564-8632	564-8632

PENNSYLVANIA:

4th MC District	19112	(215) 897-6303	897-6303
Carlisle Barracks	17013	(717) 245-3131	245-3839
Defense Industrial Supply Ctr	19111	(215) 697-2000	697-2000
Defense Personnel Center	19101	(215) 737-2000	737-2314
Fort Indiantown Gap	17003	(717) 861-2000	861-2000
Kelley Support Center	15071	(693) 777-1173	777-6770
Letterkenny Army Depot	17201	(717) 267-8111	267-8111
Mechanicsburg Def Depot	17055	(717) 790-2000	770-6770
N. Cumberland			
Defense Distribution	17070	(717) 770-6011	770-6770
Naval Aviation Supply Office	19111	(215) 697-2000	697-2000
Naval Ships Parts Center	17055	(717) 790-2000	790-2000
PA ANG HQ	17003	(717) 861-8500	861-8500
Philadelphia Naval Base	19112	(215) 897-5000	897-5000
Tobyhanna Army Depot	18466	(717) 895-7000	895-7000

CG Marine Safety Group	19147	(215) 271-4800	271-4800
Warminster Naval Air Warfare Center	18974	(215) 441-2000	441-2000
Willow Grove NAS Joint Reserve Base	19090	(215) 443-1000	443-1000

RHODE ISLAND:

Coventry ANG Station	02816	(401) 392-0800	392-0800
Newport Naval Education & Training Center	02841	(401) 841-3456	841-3456
Rhode Island ANG HQ	02904	(401) 457-4100	457-4100

SOUTH CAROLINA:

Beaufort MC Air Station	29904	(803) 522-7100	522-7100
Beaufort Naval Hospital	29902	(803) 525-5600	525-5582
Charleston AFB	29405	(800) 438-2694	566-3282
Charleston Coast Guard Base	29401	(803) 724-7600	724-7600
Charleston Naval Base	29408	(803) 743-4111	743-4111
Charleston NWS	29408	(803) 743-4111	743-4111
Fort Jackson	29207	(803) 751-7511	751-7671
McEntire ANGB	29044	(803) 776-5121	776-5121
Parris Island Marine Corps Recruit Depot	29905	(803) 525-2111	525-3358
Shaw AFB	29152	(803) 668-8110	668-2811

SOUTH DAKOTA:

Ellsworth AFB	57706	(605) 385-1000	385-1379
Foss Field ANG Base	57117	(605) 333-5700	333-5700

TENNESSEE:

Arnold Air Station	37389	(615) 454-3000	454-3000
McGhee Tyson ANG Base	37642	(800) 524-5735	524-5735
Memphis Defense Depot	38114	(901) 775-6011	775-6011
Memphis Naval Air Station	38054	(901) 873-5509	873-5509

TEXAS:

Beaumont Army Medical Ctr	79920	(915) 569-2121	569-2909
Brooke Army Medical Ctr	78234	(210) 916-3400	916-3400
Brooks AFB	78235	(210) 536-1110	536-1841
Camp Bullis	78234	(210) 221-7510	221-3302
Camp Stanley	78015	(210) 221-7403	221-7403
Camp Swift	78602	(512) 321-2497	321-2497

Corpus Christi Army Depot	78419	(512) 939-2411	939-2411
Corpus Christi CGAS	78419	(512) 939-2070	939-2070
Corpus Christi NAS	78419	(512) 939-2811	939-2384
Dallas Naval Air Station	75211	(214) 266-6111	266-6640
Dyess AFB	79607	(915) 696-0212	696-3098
El Dorado AFS	76936	(915) 654-4273	654-4273
Ellington Field ANG Base	77034	(713) 929-2110	929-2110
Fort Bliss	79916	(915) 568-2121	568-1113
Fort Hood	76544	(817) 287-1110	287-1110
Fort Sam Houston	78234	(210) 221-1211	221-3302
Ft. Worth NAS			
Joint Reserve Base	76127	(817) 782-5000	782-5000
Galveston Coast Guard Base	77553	(409) 766-5623	766-5623
Garland ANG Station	75046	(214) 530-2575	530-2575
Goodfellow AFB	76908	(915) 654-3231	654-3410
Houston CGAS	77034	(713) 481-0025	481-0025
Ingleside Naval Station	78362	(512) 776-4200	776-4200
Kelly AFB	78241	(210) 925-1110	925-1110
Kingsville Naval Air Station	78363	(512) 595-6136	595-6136
La Porte ANG Station	77571	(713) 471-5111	471-5111
Lackland AFB	78236	(210) 671-1110	671-1110
Laughlin AFB	78843	(210) 298-3511	298-3511
Nederland ANG Stn	77705	(409) 727-1387	727-1387
Randolph AFB	78150	(210) 652-1110	652-1841
Red River Army Depot	75507	(903) 334-2141	334-2185
Reese AFB	79489	(806) 885-4511	885-3276
Sheppard AFB	76311	(817) 676-2511	676-1841
Wilford Hall Medical Ctr	78236	(210) 670-7100	670-7412
UTAH:			
Air Nat'l Guard Base	84116	(801) 595-2200	595-2200
Dugway Proving Ground	84022	(801) 831-2151	831-2151
Hill AFB	84056	(801) 777-7221	777-1845
Ogden Defense			
Distribution Depot	84407	(801) 399-7011	399-7011
Tooele Army Depot	84074	(801) 833-3211	883-2094
VIRGINIA:			
Alexandria CG Information			
Systems Center	22310	(703) 313-5400	313-5400
Cheaspeake Naval Security	23322	(804) 421-8000	614-3155*

Cheatham Annex Naval Supply Center	23187	(804) 887-4000	614-3155*
Dam Neck Fleet Combat Training Center–Atlantic	23461	(804) 433-6234	614-3155*
Fort A. P. Hill	22427	(804) 633-8710	633-8428
Fort Belvoir	22060	(703) 545-6700	805-2043
Fort Eustis	23604	(804) 878-1212	878-5215
Fort Lee	23801	(804) 734-1011	734-6855
Fort Monroe	23651	(804) 727-2111	727-2111
Fort Myer	22211	(703) 545-6700	545-6700
Fort Pickett	23824	(804) 292-8621	292-2266
Fort Story	23459	(804) 422-7305	422-7682
Henderson Hall	22214	(703) 545-6700	614-2344
JAG School	22903	(804) 972-6300	972-6300
Langley AFB	23665	(804) 764-9990	764-5615
Little Creek NAB	23521	(804) 444-0000	614-3155*
Naval Surface Warfare Ctr	22448	(540) 653-8531	653-8531
Norfolk NAS	23511	(804) 444-0000	614-3155*
Norfolk Naval Station	23511	(804) 444-0000	614-3155*
Norfolk Navy Shipyard	23709	(804) 396-3000	614-3155*
Oceana NAS	23460	(804) 444-0000	614-3155*
Portsmouth CG Support Ctr	23703	(804) 686-4002	483-8586
Portsmouth Naval Hospital	23708	(804) 398-5008	398-5008
Quantico Marine Corps Combat Command	22134	(540) 640-2121	640-2121
Vint Hill Farms Station	22186	(540) 349-6000	349-5864
Virginia ANG HQ	23150	(804) 236-6000	236-6000
Yorktown CG Reserve Trng	23690	(804) 898-3500	898-2181
Yorktown Naval Weapons Stn	23691	(804) 887-4000	614-3155*

*Area code (202). These installations do not have base locators, the number listed is the Navy World Wide Locator.

WASHINGTON:

Bangor NSB	98315	(360) 396-6111	396-5733
Bremerton Naval Hospital	98312	(360) 479-6600	479-6600
Everett Naval Station	98207	(206) 304-3000	304-4206
Fairchild AFB	99011	(509) 247-1212	247-5875
Fort Lewis	98433	(206) 967-1110	967-6221
McChord AFB	98438	(206) 984-1910	984-1910
Naval Station Puget Sound	98314	(360) 476-3466	476-2335
Port Angeles CGAS	98362	(360) 457-2226	457-2226

Seattle CG Support Center	98134	(206) 217-6100	217-6100
Seattle ANG Base	98108	(206) 764-5600	764-5600
Washington ANG HQ	98430	(206) 512-8000	512-8000
Whidbey Island NAS	98278	(206) 257-2211	257-2631

WEST VIRGINIA:

Sugar Grove Naval Security	26815	(304) 249-6304	249-6304
West Virginia ANG HQ	25311	(304) 341-6300	341-6300

WISCONSIN:

Fort McCoy	54656	(608) 388-2222	388-2222
Milwaukee CG Group	53207	(414) 747-7100	747-7100
Mitchell Field	53207	(414) 482-5000	482-5000
Volk Field ANG Base	54618	(608) 427-3341	427-3341

WYOMING:

Camp Guernsey	82214	(307) 836-2823	836-2823
F.E. Warren AFB	82005	(307) 775-1110	775-1841

GUAM:

Agana Naval Hospital	96637	(671) 344-9340	344-9235
Anderson AFB	96542	(671) 366-1110	366-1110
Dededo Naval Commo Stn	96919	(671) 355-5333	355-5333
Sumay Naval Station	96540	(671) 355-1110	339-7133

(Country Code: 011. Dial this before the area code.)

PUERTO RICO:

Borinquen CGAS	00604	(809) 882-3500	882-3500
Camp Santiago	00751	(809) 824-3156	824-3110
Ceiba NAS Roosevelt Road	00735	(809) 865-2000	865-3033
Fort Buchanan	00934	(809) 273-3400	273-3400
Muniz ANG Base	00904	(809) 253-5100	253-5100
Puerto Rico ANG HQ	00902	(809) 723-0395	723-0395
San Juan Coast Guard Base	00902	(809) 729-6800	729-6800

Air Force, Army and Fleet Post Offices

The Armed Forces World-Wide Locators provide unit locations of military members assigned overseas by their post office zip codes *only*. By comparing these numbers to the following list, you can determine the overseas geographical location. If you wish to obtain the unit to which the member is assigned, write to the locator at the APO or FPO. For example:

Locator
APO AE 09001

The two-letter code AE is for APOs and FPOs in Europe. AP is for APOs and FPOs in the Pacific area. AA is for APOs and FPOs in Central or South America. Following are some examples of military addresses in proper format:

Sgt. John Doe
Company A, 122 Signal Battalion
Unit 20501, Box 4290
APO AE 09795

PCCM John Doe
HI Division, Admin
USS Nimitz (CVN 88)
FPO AP 96697

1st Lt. John Doe
Company A, 111 Maintenance Battalion
APO AA 34002

APOs and FPOs for Europe, Africa, and Middle East

APO	AE	09007	Heidelberg, Germany
APO	AE	09009	Ramstein, Germany
APO	AE	09012	Ramstein, Germany
APO	AE	09014	Heidelberg, Germany
APO	AE	09021	Kapaun, Germany
APO	AE	09028	Sandhofen, Germany
APO	AE	09031	Kitzingen, Germany
APO	AE	09033	Schweinfurt, Germany
APO	AE	09034	Baumholder, Germany
APO	AE	09036	Wurzburg, Germany
APO	AE	09042	Schwetzingen, Germany
APO	AE	09045	Kirchgoens, Germany
APO	AE	09046	Boblingen, Germany
APO	AE	09050	Rhein Main, Germany
APO	AE	09053	Garmisch, Germany
APO	AE	09054	Kaiserslautern, Germany
APO	AE	09056	Worms, Germany
APO	AE	09058	Worms, Germany
APO	AE	09059	Miesau, Germany
APO	AE	09060	Frankfurt AMT, Germany
APO	AE	09063	Heidelberg, Germany
APO	AE	09067	Kaiserslautern, Germany
APO	AE	09069	Bremerhaven, Germany
APO	AE	09072	Kerpen, Germany
APO	AE	09074	Friedberg, Germany
APO	AE	09076	Buldingen, Germany
APO	AE	09080	Bonn, Germany
APO	AE	09081	Schwetzingen, Germany
APO	AE	09086	Kaefertal, Germany
APO	AE	09089	Babenhausen, Germany
APO	AE	09090	Roedelheim, Germany
APO	AE	09094	Ramstein, Germany
APO	AE	09095	Germersheim, Germany
APO	AE	09096	Wiesbaden, Germany
APO	AE	09097	Rhein Main, Germany
APO	AE	09098	Bad Aibling, Germany
APO	AE	09099	Heidelberg, Germany
APO	AE	09100	Heidelberg, Germany
APO	AE	09102	Heidelberg, Germany
APO	AE	09103	Rhinedahlen, Germany

APO	AE	09104	Geilenkirchen, Germany
APO	AE	09107	Mohringen, Germany
APO	AE	09110	Dexheim, Germany
APO	AE	09111	Bad Kreuznach, Germany
APO	AE	09112	Sorghof, Germany
APO	AE	09114	Grafenwohr, Germany
APO	AE	09123	Spangdahlem AB, Germany
APO	AE	09126	Spangdahlem AB, Germany
APO	AE	09128	Vaihingen, Germany
APO	AE	09131	Vaihingen, Germany
APO	AE	09136	Sembach AB, Germany
APO	AE	09137	Bitburg, Germany
APO	AE	09138	Pirmasens, Germany
APO	AE	09139	Bamberg, Germany
APO	AE	09140	Illesheim, Germany
APO	AE	09142	Sembach, Germany
APO	AE	09143	Giessen, Germany
APO	AE	09154	Stuttgart, Germany
APO	AE	09157	Augsburg, Germany
APO	AE	09165	Hanau, Germany
APO	AE	09166	Mannheim, Germany
APO	AE	09169	Geissen, Germany
APO	AE	09172	Oberammergau, Germany
APO	AE	09173	Hohenfels, Germany
APO	AE	09175	Darmstadt, Germany
APO	AE	09177	Ansbach, Germany
APO	AE	09178	Augsburg, Germany
APO	AE	09180	Landstuhl, Germany
APO	AE	09182	Giebelstadt, Germany
APO	AE	09183	Mannheim, Germany
APO	AE	09185	Mainz, Germany
APO	AE	09189	Pirmasens, Germany
APO	AE	09211	Darmstadt, Germany
APO	AE	09212	Rhein Main AB, Germany
APO	AE	09213	Frankfurt, Germany
APO	AE	09214	Buchel AB, Germany
APO	AE	09220	Wiesbaden, Germany
APO	AE	09225	Kitzingen, Germany
APO	AE	09226	Schweinfurt, Germany
APO	AE	09227	Kaiserslautern, Germany
APO	AE	09229	Kaiserslautern, Germany
APO	AE	09237	Frankfurt, Germany

APO	AE	09244	Wurzburg, Germany
APO	AE	09245	Nurnberg, Germany
APO	AE	09250	Katterbach, Germany
APO	AE	09252	Bad Kreuznach, Germany
APO	AE	09262	Idar-Oberstein, Germany
APO	AE	09263	Kaiserslautern, Germany
APO	AE	09264	Ansbach, Germany
APO	AE	09265	Berlin, Germany
APO	AE	09266	Sechkenheim, Germany
APO	AE	09267	Mannheim, Germany
APO	AE	09396	Incirlik, Ramstein AB, Germany
APO	AE	09409	St. Mawgan, England
FPO	AE	09419	Edzell, Scotland
FPO	AE	09420	Brawdy, Wales
FPO	AE	09421	London, England
APO	AE	09447	Bedford, England
APO	AE	09448	RAF Burtonwood, England
APO	AE	09449	Uxbridge, England
APO	AE	09454	Cheltenham, England
APO	AE	09456	RAF Fairford, England
APO	AE	09459	Bury-St. Edmunds, Suffolk, England
APO	AE	09461	Thetford, England
APO	AE	09463	Bedford Amt, England
APO	AE	09464	RAF Lakenheath, England
APO	AE	09465	Shefford Bedfordshire, England
APO	AE	09468	Harrogate, England
APO	AE	09469	RAF Alconbury, Cambridgeshire, England
APO	AE	09470	Huntingdon, Cambridge, England
APO	AE	09494	RAF Croughton, Newhamptonshire, England
APO	AE	09496	Fylingdale, Yorkshire, England
FPO	AE	09498	London, England
FPO	AE	09499	London, England
FPO	AE	09508	Guantanamo Bay, Cuba
FPO	AE	09593	Guantanamo Bay, Cuba
FPO	AE	09596	Guantanamo Bay, Cuba
APO	AE	09601	Aviano AB, Italy
FPO	AE	09609	Gaeta, Italy
APO	AE	09610	Ghedi AB, Italy
FPO	AE	09612	LaMaddelena Sardinia, Italy
APO	AE	09613	Livorno, Italy

FPO	AE	09619	Naples, Italy
FPO	AE	09620	Naples, Italy
FPO	AE	09621	Naples, Italy
FPO	AE	09622	Naples, Italy
FPO	AE	09623	Sigonella, Italy
APO	AE	09624	Rome, Italy
FPO	AE	09625	Naples, Italy
FPO	AE	09626	Naples, Italy
FPO	AE	09627	Sigonella, Italy
APO	AE	09628	Verona, Italy
APO	AE	09630	Vicenza, Italy
APO	AE	09631	Sigonella, Italy
APO	AE	09642	Madrid, Spain
APO	AE	09643	Moron AB, Spain
FPO	AE	09644	Rota, Spain
FPO	AE	09645	Rota, Spain
APO	AE	09647	Torrejon AB, Spain
APO	AE	09703	Brunssum, Netherlands
APO	AE	09704·	Thule AB, Greenland
APO	AE	09705	Shape Casteau, Belgium
APO	AE	09706	Stavanger, Norway
APO	AE	09707	Oslo, Norway
APO	AE	09708	Chievres AB, Belgium
APO	AE	09713	Maastricht, Netherlands
APO	AE	09714	Brussels City, Belgium
APO	AE	09715	The Hague, Netherlands
APO	AE	09716	Copenhagen, Denmark
APO	AE	09717	Volkel, Netherlands
APO	AE	09718	Rabat, Morocco
APO	AE	09720	Terceira, Azores, Portugal
APO	AE	09721	Helsinki, Finland
APO	AE	09722	Karup, Denmark
APO	AE	09723	Helsinki, Finland
APO	AE	09724	Brussels, Belgium
APO	AE	09725	AFI Keflavik, Iceland
APO	AE	09726	Lisbon, Portugal
FPO	AE	09728	Keflavik, Iceland
FPO	AE	09729	Hofn, Iceland
APO	AE	09732	North Bay, Canada
APO	AE	09777	Paris, France
APO	AE	09802	Taif, Saudi Arabia
APO	AE	09803	Riyadh, Saudi Arabia

APO	AE	09804	Dhahran, Saudi Arabia
APO	AE	09805	Al-Jubail, Saudi Arabia
APO	AE	09808	Dhahran, Saudi Arabia
APO	AE	09809	Khamis Mushayt, Saudi Arabia
APO	AE	09810	Tabuk, Saudi Arabia
APO	AE	09811	Jeddah, Saudi Arabia
APO	AE	09812	Islamabad, Pakistan
APO	AE	09813	Monrovia, Liberia
APO	AE	09814	Karachi, Pakistan
APO	AE	09815	Mahe, India
APO	AE	09816	Balikisir, Turkey
APO	AE	09819	Izmir, Turkey
APO	AE	09821	Izmir, Turkey
APO	AE	09822	Ankara, Turkey
APO	AE	09823	Ankara, Turkey
APO	AE	09824	Adana, Turkey
APO	AE	09825	Diyarbakir, Turkey
APO	AE	09827	Istanbul, Turkey
APO	AE	09828	Kinshasa, Congo
APO	AE	09829	Khartoum, Sudan
APO	AE	09830	Tel Aviv, Israel
APO	AE	09831	Nairobi, Kenya
APO	AE	09832	El Gorah, Egypt
APO	AE	09833	Sharm El Shiek, Egypt
FPO	AE	09834	Jufair, Bahrain
FPO	AE	09835	Cairo, Egypt
FPO	AE	09836	Nicosia, Cypress
APO	AE	09839	Cairo, Egypt
APO	AE	09841	Athens, Greece
APO	AE	09842	Athens, Greece
APO	AE	09843	Araxos, Greece
APO	AE	09852	Riyadh, Saudi Arabia
APO	AE	09853	Al-Dharfa U AE, Saudi Arabia
APO	AE	09855	Kuwait City, Kuwait
APO	AE	09858	Daharan, Saudi Arabia
APO	AE	09859	Tabuk, Saudi Arabia
APO	AE	09861	Khamis-Mushayt, Saudi Arabia
APO	AE	09863	Riyadh, Saudi Arabia
APO	AE	09864	Riyadh, Saudi Arabia
FPO	AE	09865	Souda Bay, Crete, Greece
APO	AE	09866	Jufair, Bahrain
APO	AE	09868	Cairo, Egypt

APO	AE 09871	Riyadh, Saudi Arabia
APO	AE 09873	Tabuk, Saudi Arabia
APO	AE 09875	Al Ain UAD, Saudi Arabia
APO	AE 09876	Thumrait Oman, Saudi Arabia
APO	AE 09877	Mastrah Oman, Saudi Arabia
APO	AE 09878	Cairo West, Egypt
APO	AE 09880	Kuwait City, Kuwait
APO	AE 09881	Eskan Village, Saudi Arabia
APO	AE 09889	Kuwait City, Kuwait
APO	AE 09891	Bateen U AE, Saudi Arabia
APO	AE 09892	Amman, Jordon
APO	AE 09894	Dhahran, Saudi Arabia
APO	AE 09896	Taif, Saudi Arabia
APO	AE 09897	Bahrain, Saudi Arabia
APO	AE 09898	Doha Gatar, Saudi Arabia
APO	AE 09899	Mombasa, Kenya

Central and South America

APO	AA 34001	Howard AFB, Panama
APO	AA 34002	Albrook AFS, Panama
APO	AA 34003	Quarry Heights, Panama
APO	AA 34004	Fort Clayton, Panama
APO	AA 34005	Fort Wm. D. Davis, Panama
APO	AA 34006	Fort Kobbe, Panama
APO	AA 34007	Fort Amador, Panama
APO	AA 34009	Albrook AFS, Panama
APO	AA 34011	Albrook AFS, Panama
APO	AA 34012	Panama City, Panama
APO	AA 34021	Managua, Nicaragua
APO	AA 34022	Tegucigalpa, Honduras
APO	AA 34023	San Salvador, El Salvador
APO	AA 34024	Guatemala City, Guatemala
APO	AA 34025	Belize City, Belize
APO	AA 34030	Rio de Janiero, Brazil
APO	AA 34031	Lima, Peru
APO	AA 34032	La Paz, Bolivia
APO	AA 34033	Santiago, Chile
APO	AA 34034	Buenas Aires, Argentina
APO	AA 34035	Montivideo, Uraguay
APO	AA 34036	Asuncion, Paraguay
APO	AA 34037	Caracas, Venezuela
APO	AA 34038	Bogota, Colombia

APO	AA	34039	Quito, Ecuador
APO	AA	34040	San Juan, Puerto Rico
APO	AA	34041	Santo Domingo, Dominican Rep
APO	AA	34042	Comayagua, Honduras
APO	AA	34047	Albrook AFS, El Salvador
FPO	AA	34050	Borinquen, Puerto Rico
FPO	AA	34051	Roosevelt Roads, Puerto Rico
FPO	AA	34053	Sabana Seca, Puerto Rico
FPO	AA	34055	Bridgetown, Barbados
FPO	AA	34058	Andros Island, The Bahamas
FPO	AA	34060	Galetta Island, Panama
FPO	AA	34061	Rodman, Panama
FPO	AA	34077	Port-au-Prince, Haiti

Pacific Area

APO	AP	96201	Kimpo, Korea
APO	AP	96203	Yongsan, Korea
APO	AP	96204	Yongsan, Korea
APO	AP	96205	Yongsan, Korea
APO	AP	96206	Yongsan, Korea
APO	AP	96207	Yongsan, Korea
APO	AP	96208	Chunchon, Korea
APO	AP	96212	Taegu, Korea
APO	AP	96214	Kimhae, Korea
APO	AP	96215	Pohang, Korea
APO	AP	96217	Pohang, Korea
APO	AP	96218	Taegu, Korea
APO	AP	96219	Pohang, Korea
APO	AP	96220	Cheju-Do, Korea
APO	AP	96221	Pohang, Korea
APO	AP	96224	Tongduchon-ni, Korea
APO	AP	96251	Yong-Tae-Ri, Korea
APO	AP	96257	Uijongbu, Korea
APO	AP	96258	Uijongbu, Korea
APO	AP	96259	Pusan, Korea
APO	AP	96260	Waegwan, Korea
APO	AP	96262	Kwang Ju AB, Korea
APO	AP	96264	Kunsan AB, Korea
APO	AP	96266	Osan AB, Korea
APO	AP	96267	Osan AB, Korea
FPO	AP	96269	Chinha, Korea
APO	AP	96271	Pyongtaek, Korea

APO	AP	96275	Suwon, Korea
APO	AP	96276	Seoul, Korea
APO	AP	96278	Song Tansi, Korea
APO	AP	96283	Bupyeong, Korea
APO	AP	96284	Bupyeong, Korea
APO	AP	96297	Wongju, Kangwon-Do, Korea
FPO	AP	96306	Atsugi, Japan
FPO	AP	96309	Osaka, Japan
FPO	AP	96310	Iwakuni, Japan
FPO	AP	96313	Kami Seya, Japan
APO	AP	96319	Misawa AB, Japan
FPO	AP	96321	Sasebo, Japan
FPO	AP	96322	Sasebo, Japan
APO	AP	96323	Yokota AB, Japan
APO	AP	96325	Yokota AB, Japan
APO	AP	96326	Yokota AB, Japan
APO	AP	96328	Yokota AB, Japan
APO	AP	96330	Yokota AB, Japan
APO	AP	96336	Tokyo, Japan
APO	AP	96337	Tokyo, Japan
APO	AP	96338	Tokyo, Japan
APO	AP	96339	Camp Zama, Japan
APO	AP	96343	Tokyo, Japan
FPO	AP	96347	Yokohama, Japan
FPO	AP	96348	Yokohama, Japan (Housing Area)
FPO	AP	96349	Yokosuka, Japan (FLT ACT)
FPO	AP	96350	Yokosuka (NAVHOSP), Japan
FPO	AP	96362	Camp Kuwae (NRMC), Okinawa, Japan
APO	AP	96364	Kadena AB, Okinawa, Japan
APO	AP	96365	Naha, Okinawa, Japan
APO	AP	96367	Kadena AB, Okinawa, Japan
APO	AP	96368	Kadena AB, Okinawa, Japan
FPO	AP	96370	Naha, Okinawa, Japan
FPO	AP	96372	Futema, Okinawa, Japan
FPO	AP	96373	Makiminato, Okinawa, Japan
APO	AP	96374	Makiminato, Okinawa, Japan
APO	AP	96375	Makiminato, Okinawa, Japan
APO	AP	96376	Yomitan, Okinawa, Japan
FPO	AP	96377	Tengan, Okinawa, Japan
APO	AP	96378	Makiminato, Okinawa, Japan
APO	AP	96379	Zukeran, Okinawa, Japan
APO	AP	96384	Camp Hansen, Japan

APO	AP 96386	MCAS Futenma, Japan
APO	AP 96387	Camp Fuji, Japan
APO	AP 96388	Camp Schwab, Japan
APO	AP 96440	Manila, Luzon, Philippines
FPO	AP 96464	Diego Garcia Isl, Diego Garcia
FPO	AP 96505	Adak, (NAVCOMMSTA) Alaska
FPO	AP 96506	Adak, Alaska
APO	AP 96508	Fort Greely, Big Delta, Alaska
APO	AP 96511	Masset, B.C., Canada
APO	AP 96512	Shemya AFB, Alaska
FPO	AP 96516	Midway Islands
APO	AP 96518	Wake Island
APO	AP 96520	Jakarta, Indonesia
FPO	AP 96521	Hong Kong, BCC
FPO	AP 96522	Hong Kong, BCC
FPO	AP 96529	Brisbane, Australia
FPO	AP 96530	Perth, Australia
FPO	AP 96531	Christchurch, New Zealand
FPO	AP 96534	Singapore
FPO	AP 96535	Kuala Lumpur, Malaysia
FPO	AP 96536	Agana (COMNAV), Guam
FPO	AP 96537	Agana (NCTAMS WESTPAC), Guam
FPO	AP 96538	Agana (NAVHOSP), Guam
FPO	AP 96539	Agana, Guam, (NAS) Marianas Islands
FPO	AP 96540	Agana, Guam, (NAVSTA) Marianas Islands
APO	AP 96541	Agana, (NAVMAG), Guam
APO	AP 96542	Andersen AFB, Guam
APO	AP 96543	Agana, Guam
APO	AP 96546	Bangkok, Thailand
APO	AP 96547	Bangkok (PACAFAIRPS), Thailand
APO	AP 96548	Alice Springs, Australia
APO	AP 96549	Canberra A.C.T., Australia
APO	AP 96550	Exmouth, Australia
APO	AP 96551	Melbourne, Victoria, Australia
APO	AP 96552	Woomera, Australia
APO	AP 96553	Sydney, Australia
APO	AP 96554	Sydney, Australia
APO	AP 96555	Kwajalein, Marshall Isands
APO	AP 96556	Pohakuloa, Hawaii
APO	AP 96557	Kwaja Atoll, Marshall Islands
APO	AP 96558	Johnson Island, Hawaii
FPO	AP 96598	Amundsen-Scott, Antarctica
FPO	AP 96599	McMurdo Station, Antarctica

U.S. Coast Guard Ships

Ship's Name	Hull Number	Zip Code
USCGC Basswood	WLB 388	AP 96661–3901
USCGC Boutwell	WHEC 719	AP 96661–3902
USCGC Galveston Is	WPB 1349	AP 96450–1056
USCGC Jarvis	WHEC 725	AP 96669–3912
USCGC Mallow	WLB 396	AP 96672–3913
USCGC Mellon	WHEC 717	AP 96698–3914
USCGC Midgett	WHEC 726	AP 96698–3915
USCGC Morgenthau	WHEC 722	AP 96672–3916
USCGC Munro	WHEC 724	AP 96672–3917
USCGC Nunivak	WPB 1306	AA 34051–3823
USCGC Ocracoke	WPB 1307	AA 34051–3823
USCGC Polar Sea	WAGB 11	AP 96698–3919
USCGC Polar Star	WAGB 10	AP 96698–3920
USCGC Rush	WHEC 723	AP 96677–3921
USCGC Sassafras	WLB 401	AP 96678–3922
USCGC Sherman	WHEC 720	AP 96678–3923
USCGC Vashon	WPB 1308	AA 34051–3823

U.S. Navy Ships and Homeports

The following contains active Navy ships, hull numbers, fleet post offices (zip codes), and home ports. The codes designate the assigned homeports:

0. No homeport assigned	18. New York, NY
2. Alameda, CA	19. Philadelphia, PA
3. Concord, CA	21. Charleston, SC
4. Long Beach, CA	23. Ingleside, TX
5. Oakland, CA	24. Little Creek, Norfolk, VA
6. San Diego, CA	25. Norfolk, VA
8. Vallejo, CA	26. Bangor, WA
9. Groton, CT	27. Bremerton, WA
10. New London, CT	29. Tacoma, WA
12. Mayport, FL	30. Gaeta, Italy
13. Kings Bay, GA	31. La Maddalena, Italy
14. Pearl Harbor, HI	32. Sasebo, Japan
15. Pascagoula, MS	33. Yokosuka, Japan
16. Portsmouth, NH	34. Guam, Marianas Islands
17. Earle, NJ	35. Everett, WA

Ship's Name	Hull Number	Zip Code	Home Port
Able	TAGOS 20	None Assigned	0
Alabama	SSBN 731	AP 96698-2108	26
Alaska	SSBN 732	AP 96698-2111	26
Alatna	TAOG 81	None Assigned	0
Albany	SSN 753	AE 09564-2409	25
Albuquerque	SSN 706	AE 09564-2386	9
Alexandria	SSN 757	AE 09564-2413	9
Algol	TAKR 287	None Assigned	0
Altair	TAKR 291	None Assigned	0
America	CV 66	AE 09531-2790	25
American Condor	TAKR 9673	None Assigned	0
American Cormorant	TAK 2062	None Assigned	0
American Falcon	TAKR 9672	None Assigned	0
American Merlin	TAK 9302	None Assigned	0
American Osprey	TAOT 5075	None Assigned	0
Anderson James Jr., Pfc.	TAK 3002	None Assigned	0
Anchorage	LSD 36	AP 96660-1724	6
Annapolis	SSN 760	AE 09564-2416	9
Antares	TAKR 294	None Assigned	0
Antietam	CG 54	AP 96660-1174	4
Antrim	FFG 20	AA 34090-1476	15
Anzio	CG 68	AE 09564-1188	25
Apache	TATF 172	None Assigned	0
Archerfish	SSN 678	AE 09564-2358	9
Ardent	MCM 12	AA 34090-1932	23
Arkansas	CGN 41	AP 96660-1168	2
Artic	AOE 8	AE 09564-3039	25
Asheville	SSN 758	AP 96660-2414	6
Ashland	LSD 48	AE 09564-1736	24
Assertive	TAGOS 9	None Assigned	0
Atlanta	SSN 712	AE 09564-2392	25
Augusta	SSN 710	AE 09564-2390	9
Austin	LPD 4	AE 09564-1707	25
Austral Rainbow	TAK 1005	None Assigned	0
Avenger	MCM 1	AA 34090-1921	23
Bainbridge	CGN 25	AE 09565-1161	25
Baltimore	SSN 704	AE 09565-2384	25
Banner	TAK 5008	None Assigned	0
Barry	DDG 52	AE 09565-1270	25

Ship's Name	Hull Number	Zip Code	Home Port
Bates, William H.	SSN 680	AP 96661-2360	14
Batfish	SSN 681	AE 09565-2361	9
Baugh, William B., Pfc.	TAK 3001	None Assigned	0
Beaufort	ATS 2	AP 96661-3218	32
Bellatrix	TAKR 288	None Assigned	0
Belleau Wood	LHA 3	AP 96623-1610	32
Bent, Silas	TAGS 26	None Assigned	0
Big Horn	TAO 198	None Assigned	0
Billfish	SSN 676	AE 09565-2356	9
Birmingham	SSN 695	AP 96661-2375	14
Blue Ridge	LCC 19	AP 96628-3300	33
Bluefish	SSN 675	AA 34090-2355	14
Bobo, John P., 2nd Lt.	TAK 3008	None Assigned	0
Boise	SSN 764	AE 09565-2420	25
Bold	TAGOS 12	None Assigned	0
Bonnyman, Alex, 1st Lt.	TAK 3003	None Assigned	0
Boone	FFG 28	AA 34093-1484	12
Boston	SSN 703	AE 09565-2383	9
Boxer	LHD 4	AP 96661-1663	6
Bradley, Robert G.	FFG 49	AA 34090-1503	21
Bremerton	SSN 698	AP 96661-2378	14
Briscoe	DD 977	AE 09565-1215	25
Brunswick	ATS 3	AP 96661-3219	32
Buck, Paul	TAOT 1122	None Assigned	0
Buffalo	SSN 715	AP 96661-2395	14
Buffalo Soldier	TAK 9301	None Assigned	0
Bunker Hill	CG 52	AP 96661-1172	33
Burke, Arleigh	DDG 51	AE 09565-1269	25
Butte	AE 27	AE 09565-3005	17
Button, William R., Sgt.	TAK 3012	None Assigned	0
Cable, Frank	AS 40	AA 34086-2615	21
California	CGN 36	AP 96662-1163	27
Callaghan	DDG 994	AP 96662-1266	6
Callaghan, W. M., Adm	TAKR 1001	None Assigned	0
Camden	AOE 2	AP 98799-3013	27
Capable	TAGOS 16	None Assigned	0
Cape Alava	TAK 5012	None Assigned	0
Cape Alexander	TAK 5010	None Assigned	0
Cape Ann	TAK 5009	None Assigned	0

Ship's Name	Hull Number	Zip Code	Home Port
Cape Archway	TAK 5011	None Assigned	0
Cape Avinof	TAK 5013	None Assigned	0
Cape Blanco	TAK 5060	None Assigned	0
Cape Bon	TAK 5059	None Assigned	0
Cape Borda	TAK 5058	None Assigned	0
Cape Bover	TAK 5057	None Assigned	0
Cape Breton	TAK 5056	None Assigned	0
Cape Carthage	TAK 5042	None Assigned	0
Cape Catawba	TAK 5074	None Assigned	0
Cape Chalmers	TAK 5036	None Assigned	0
Cape Clear	TAK 5039	None Assigned	0
Cape Cod	TAK 5041	None Assigned	0
Cape Decision	TAKR 5054	None Assigned	0
Cape Diamond	TAKR 5055	None Assigned	0
Cape Domingo	TAKR 5053	None Assigned	0
Cape Douglas	TAKR 5052	None Assigned	0
Cape Ducato	TAKR 5051	None Assigned	0
Cape Edmont	TAKR 5069	None Assigned	0
Cape Farewell	TAK 5073	None Assigned	0
Cape Fear	TAK 5061	None Assigned	0
Cape Flattery	TAK 5070	None Assigned	0
Cape Florida	TAK 5071	None Assigned	0
Cape Gibson	TAK 5051	None Assigned	0
Cape Girardeau	TAK 2039	None Assigned	0
Cape Henry	TAKR 5067	None Assigned	0
Cape Horn	TAKR 5068	None Assigned	0
Cape Hudson	TAKR 5066	None Assigned	0
Cape Inscription	TAKR 5076	None Assigned	0
Cape Intrepid	TAKR 11	None Assigned	0
Cape Isabel	TAKR 5062	None Assigned	0
Cape Island	TAKR 10	None Assigned	0
Cape Jacob	TAK 5029	None Assigned	0
Cape John	TAK 5022	None Assigned	0
Cape Johnson	TAK 5075	None Assigned	0
Cape Juby	TAK 5077	None Assigned	0
Cape Lambert	TAKR 5077	None Assigned	0
Cape Lobos	TAKR 5078	None Assigned	0
Cape May	TAK 5063	None Assigned	0
Cape Mendocino	TAK 5064	None Assigned	0

Ship's Name	Hull Number	Zip Code	Home Port
Cape Mohican	TAK 5065	None Assigned	0
Cape Nome	TAK 1014	None Assigned	0
Cape Orlando	TAKR 2044	None Assigned	0
Cape Race	TAKR 9960	None Assigned	0
Cape Ray	TAKR 9679	None Assigned	0
Cape Rise	TAKR 9678	None Assigned	0
Cape St George	CG 71	AE 09566-1191	25
Cape Taylor	TAKR 113	None Assigned	0
Cape Texas	TAKR 112	None Assigned	0
Cape Trinity	TAKR 9711	None Assigned	0
Cape Victory	TAKR 9701	None Assigned	0
Cape Vincent	TAKR 9666	None Assigned	0
Cape Washington	TAKR 9961	None Assigned	0
Cape Wrath	TAKR 9962	None Assigned	0
Capella	TAKR 293	None Assigned	0
Caron	DD 970	AE 09566-1208	25
Carr	FFG 52	AA 34090-1506	21
Catawba	TATF 168	None Assigned	0
Cavalla	SSN 684	AP 96662-2364	14
Champion	MCM 4	AA 34090-1924	23
Chancellorsville	CG 62	AP 96662-1182	6
Chandler	DDG 996	AP 96662-1268	6
Charlotte	SSN 766	AP 96662-2422	14
Chattahoochee	TAOG 82	None Assigned	0
Chesapeake	TAOT 5084	None Assigned	0
Chicago	SSN 721	AP 96662-2401	6
Chief	MCM 14	AA 34090-1934	23
Chinook	PC 9	AE 09566-1968	24
Chosin	CG 65	AP 96662-1185	14
Cimarron	AO 177	AP 96662-3018	14
City of Corpus Christi	SSN 705	AE 09566-2385	9
Clark	FFG 11	AE 09566-1469	25
Cleveland	LPD 7	AP96662-1710	6
Cleveland	TAK 851	None Assing ed	0
Cobb, Samuel L.	TAOT 1123	None Assigned	0
Columbia	SSN 771	AE 09566-2425	0
Columbus	SSN 762	AP 96662-2418	14
Comet	TAKR 7	None Assigned	0
Comfort	TAH 20	None Assigned	0

Ship's Name	Hull Number	Zip Code	Home Port
Comstock	LSD 45	AP 96662-1733	6
Comte De Grasse	DD 974	AE 09566-1212	25
Concord	TAFS 5	None Assigned	0
Conolly	DD 979	AE 09566-1217	25
Constellation	CV 64	AP 96635-2780	6
Copeland	FFG 25	AP 96662-1481	6
Cornhusker State	TACS 6	None Assigned	0
Coronado	AGF 11	AP 96662-3330	6
Corpus Christie	TAK 12	None Assigned	0
Courier	TAK 5019	None Assigned	0
Courier	TAOT 10C7	AP 96662	0
Cowpens	CG 63	AP 96662-1183	6
Crommelin	FFG 37	AP 96662-1492	14
Curtiss	TAVB 4	None Assigned	0
Curts	FFG 38	AP 96662-1493	33
Cushing	DD 985	AP 96662-1223	14
Cyclone	PC 1	AE 09566-1960	24
Dallas	SSN 700	AE 09567-2380	9
Darnell, Gus W.	TAOT 1121	None Assigned	0
Davis, Rodney M.	FFG 60	AP 96663-1514	33
Defender	MCM 2	AA 34090-1922	23
Denebola	TAKR 289	None Assigned	0
Denver	LPD 9	AP 96663-1712	6
Detroit	AOE 4	AE 09567-3015	17
Devastator	MCM 6	AA 34090-1926	23
Dewert	FFG 45	AA 34090-1499	21
Dextrous	MCM 13	AA 34090-1933	23
Deyo	DD 989	AE 09567-1227	25
Diamond State	TACS 7	None Assigned	0
Diehl, Walter S.	TAO 193	None Assigned	0
Dixon	AS 37	AP 96648-2605	6
Dolphin	AGSS 555	AP 96663-4000	6
Doyle	FFG 39	AA 34090-1494	12
Dubuque	LPD 8	AP 96663-1711	32
Duchess	TAOT 1126	None Assigned	0
Duluth	LPD 6	AP 96663-1709	6
Edenton	ATS 1	AE 09568-3217	24
Effective	TAGOS 21	None Assigned	0
Eisenhower, Dwight D.	CVN 69	AE 09532-2830	25

Ship's Name	Hull Number	Zip Code	Home Port
Elliot	DD 967	AP 96664-1205	6
Elrod	FFG 55	AE 09568-1509	25
Empire State	TAP 1001	None Assigned	0
Enterprise	CVN 65	AE 09543-2810	25
Equality State	TACS 8	None Assigned	0
Ericsson, John	TAO 194	None Assigned	0
Essex	LHD 2	AP 96643-1661	6
Estocin	FFG 15	AE 09569-1473	25
Fahrion	FFG 22	AA 34091-1478	21
Fife	DD 991	AP 96665-1229	33
Finback	SSN 670	AE 09569-2350	25
Firebolt	PC 10	AE 09569-1969	24
Fitch, Aubrey	FFG 34	AA 34091-1490	12
Fitzgerald	DDG 62	AP 96665-1280	6
Flatley	FFG 21	AA 34091-1477	15
Fletcher	DD 992	AP 96665-1230	14
Flickertail State	TACS 5	None Assigned	0
Flint	TAE 32	AP 96665-3008	14
Florida	SSBN 728	AP 96698-2099	26
Ford	FFG 54	AP 96665-1508	35
Fort Fisher	LSD 40	AP 96665-1728	6
Fort Mchenry	LSD 43	AP 96665-1731	32
Foster, Paul F.	DD 964	AP 96665-1202	4
Frederick	LST 1184	AP 96665-1805	6
Gallery	FFG 26	AA 34091-1482	15
Gary	FFG 51	AP 96666-1505	6
Gates, Thomas S.	CG 51	AE 09570-1171	25
Gem State	TACS 2	None Assigned	0
Georgia	SSBN 729	AP 96698-2102	26
Germantown	LSD 42	AP 96666-1730	32
Gettysburg	CG 64	AA 34091-1184	12
Gianella, Lawrence H.	TAOT 1125	None Assigned	0
Gibson, Eric G., Sp5	TAK 5091	None Assigned	0
Gladiator	MCM 11	AA 34091-1931	23
Gopher State	TACS 4	None Assigned	0
Grand Canyon State	TACS 3	None Assigned	0
Grapple	ARS 53	AE 09570-3223	24
Grasp	ARS 51	AE 09570-3220	24
Grayling	SSN 646	AE 09570-2332	9

Ship's Name	Hull Number	Zip Code	Home Port
Green Harbour	TAK 2064	None Assigned	0
Green Mountain State	TACS 9	None Assigned	0
Green Ridge	TAK 9655	None Assigned	0
Green Valley	TAK 2049	None Assigned	0
Green Wave	TAK 2050	None Assigned	0
Groton	SSN 694	AE 09570-2374	9
Groves, Stephen W	FFG 25	AA 34091-1485	15
Grumman, Leroy	TAO 105	None Assigned	0
Guadalupe	TAO 200	None Assigned	0
Guam	LPH 9	AE 09563-1640	25
Guardian	MCM 5	AA 34091-1925	23
Gulf Banker	TAK 5044	None Assigned	0
Gulf Farmer	TAK 5045	None Assigned	0
Gulf Merchant	TAK 5046	None Assigned	0
Gulf Shipper	TAK 2035	None Assigned	0
Gulf Trader	TAK 2036	None Assigned	0
Gunston Hall	LSD 44	AE 09573-1732	24
Hall, Carter	LSD 50	None Assigned	0
Hall, John L.	FFG 32	AA 34091-1488	15
Halyburton	FFG 40	AA 34091-1495	21
Hamilton, Paul	DDG 60	AP 96667-1278	14
Hampton	SSN 767	AE 09573-2423	25
Hancock, John	DD 981	AA 34091-1219	12
Harpers Ferry	LSD 49	AP 96665-1737	0
Hartford	SSN 768	AE 09573-2424	9
Hauge, Louis J. Jr., Cpl	TAK 3000	None Assigned	0
Hawes	FFG 53	AA 34091-1507	21
Hawkbill	SSN 666	AP 96667-2346	14
Hayes	TAG 195	None Assigned	0
Hayler	DD 997	AE 09573-1231	25
Helena	SSN 725	AP 96667-2405	14
Heron	MHC 52	AA 34091-1951	23
Hewitt	DD 966	AP 96667-1204	33
Higgins, Andrew J.	TAO 190	None Assigned	0
Hill, Harry W.	DD 986	AP 96667-1224	6
Holland	AS 32	AP 96642-2585	34
Honolulu	SSN 718	AP 96667-2398	14
Houston	SSN 713	AP 96667-2393	6
Hue City	CG 66	AA 34091-1186	12

Ship's Name	Hull Number	Zip Code	Home Port
Humpreys, Joshua	TAO 188	None Assigned	0
Hurricane	PC 3	AP 96667-1962	6
Independence	CV 62	AP 96618-2760	33
Indianapolis	SSN 697	AP 96668-2377	14
Indomitable	TAGOS 7	None Assigned	0
Ingersoll	DD 990	AP 96668-1228	14
Ingraham	FFG 61	AP 96668-1515	35
Jackson, Henry M.	SSBN 730	AP 96698-2105	26
Jacksonville	SSN 699	AE 09575-2379	25
James, Reuben	FFG 57	AP 96669-1511	14
Jarrett	FFG 33	AP 96669-1489	4
Jefferson City	SSN 759	AP 96669-2415	6
Jones, John Paul	DDG 53	AP 96669-1271	0
Juneau	LPD 10	AP 96669-1713	6
Kaiser, Henry J.	TAO 187	None Assigned	0
Kalamazoo	AOR 6	AE 09576-3028	25
Kamehameha	SSN 642	AP 96670-2063	14
Kanawha	TAO 196	None Assigned	0
Kane	TAGS 27	None Assigned	0
Kauffman	FFG 59	AE 09576-1513	25
Kearsarge	LHD 3	AE 09534-1662	25
Kennedy, John F.	CV 67	AE 09538-2800	19
Kentucky	SSBN 737	AA 34091-4990	13
Key West	SSN 722	AE 09576-2402	25
Keystone State	TACS 1	None Assigned	0
Kidd	DDG 993	AE 09576-1265	25
Kilauea	TAE 26	None Assigned	0
Kingfisher	MHC 56	AA 34091-1956	23
Kinkaid	DD 965	AP 96670-1203	4
Kiska	AE 35	AP 96670-3011	3
Kitty Hawk	CV 63	AP 96634-2770	6
Klakring	FFG 42	AA 34091-1497	21
Kocak, Matej, Sgt	TAK 3005	None Assigned	0
La Jolla	SSN 701	AP 96671-2381	6
La Moure County	LST 1194	AE 09577-1815	24
La Salle	AGF 3	AE 09577-3320	25
Laboon	DDG 58	AE 09577-1276	25
Lake	TAK 5016	None Assigned	0
Lake Champlain	CG 57	AP 96671-1177	6

Ship's Name	Hull Number	Zip Code	Home Port
Lake Erie	CG 70	AP 96671-1190	14
Land, Emory S.	AS 39	AE 09545-2610	25
Leftwich	DD 984	AP 96671-1222	14
Lenthall, John	TAO 189	None Assigned	0
Leyte Gulf	CG 55	AA 34091-1175	12
Lincoln, Abraham	CVN 72	AP 96612-2872	2
Littlehales	TAGS 62	None Assigned	0
Lopez, Baleomero, 1st Lt.	TAK 3010	None Assigned	0
Los Angeles	SSN 688	AP 96671-2368	14
Louisville	SSN 724	AP 96671-2404	14
Loyal	TAGOS 22	None Assigned	0
Lummus, Jack, 1st Lt.	TAK 3011	None Assigned	0
Maersk Constellation	TAKR 2053	None Assigned	0
Maine	SSBN 741	None Assigned	0
Mars	TAFS 1	None Assigned	0
Maryland	SSBN 738	AA 34092-2129	13
Matthiesen, Richard G.	TAOT 1124	None Assigned	0
McCain, John S.	DDG 56	AP 96672-1274	14
McClusky	FFG 41	AP 96672-1496	33
McDonnell	TAGS 51	None Assigned	0
McInerney	FFG 8	AA 34092-1466	12
McKee	AS 41	AP 96621-2620	6
Memphis	SSN 691	AE 09578-2371	16
Mercy	TAH 19	None Assigned	0
Merrill	DD 976	AP 96672-1214	6
Merrimack	AO 179	AE 09578-3020	25
Meteor	TAKR 9	None Assigned	0
Miami	SSN 755	AE 09578-2411	9
Michigan	SSBN 727	AP 96698-2096	26
Minneapolis-Saint Paul	SSN 708	AE 09578-2388	25
Mission Buenaventura	TAOT 1012	None Assigned	0
Mission Capistrano	TAOT 5005	None Assigned	0
Mississippi	CGN 40	AE 09578-1167	25
Mitscher	DDG 57	AE 09578-1275	25
Mobile Bay	CG 53	AP 96672-1173	33
Mohawk	TATF 170	None Assigned	0
Monongahela	AO 178	AE 09578-3019	25
Monsoon	PC 4	AP 96672-1963	6
Monterey	CG 61	AA 34092-1181	12

Ship's Name	Hull Number	Zip Code	Home Port
Montpelier	SSN 765	AE 09578-2421	25
Moore, John A.	FFG 19	AP 96672-1475	6
Moosebrugger	DD 980	AA 34092-1218	12
Morison, Samuel Eliot	FFG 13	AA 34092-1471	21
Mount Baker	AE 34	AA 34092-3010	21
Mount Hood	AE 29	AP 96672-3007	3
Mount Vernon	LSD 39	AP 96672-1727	6
Mount Washington	TAOT 5076	None Assigned	0
Mount Whitney	LCC 20	AE 09517-3310	25
Narragansett	TATF 167	None Assigned	0
Narwhal	SSN 671	AA 34092-2351	21
Nashville	LPD 13	AE 09579-1715	25
Nassau	LHA 4	AE 09557-1615	25
Navajo	TATF 169	None Assigned	0
Nebraska	SSBN 739	AA 34092-2132	13
Nevada	SSBN 733	AP 96698-2114	26
New Orleans	LPH 11	AP 96627-1650	6
New York City	SSN 696	AP 96673-2376	14
Newport News	SSN 750	AE 09579-2406	25
Niagara Falls	AFS 3	AP 96673-3032	34
Nicholas	FFG 47	AA 34092-1501	21
Nicholson	DD 982	AA 34092-1220	21
Nimitz	CVN 68	AP 98780-2820	27
Noble Star	TAK 9653	None Assigned	0
Nodaway	TAOG 78	None Assigned	0
Norfolk	SSN 714	AE 09579-2394	25
Normandy	CG 60	AE 09579-1180	25
Northern Light	TAK 284	None Assigned	0
O'Bannon	DD 987	AA 34092-1225	21
O'Brien	DD 975	AP 96674-1213	33
Obregon, Eugene A., Pfc	TAK 3006	None Assigned	0
Observation Island	TAGM 23	None Assigned	0
Ogden	LPD 5	AP 96674-1708	6
Ohio	SSBN 726	AP 96698-2093	26
Oklahoma City	SSN 723	AE 09581-2403	25
Oldendorf	DD 972	AP 96674-1210	6
Olympia	SSN 717	AP 96674-2397	14
Oriole	MHC 55	None Assigned	0
Osprey	MHC 51	AA 34092-1950	21

Ship's Name	Hull Number	Zip Code	Home Port
Parche	SSN 683	AP 96675-2363	26
Pasadena	SSN 752	AP 96675-2408	6
Patriot	MCM 7	AA 34092-1927	23
Patriot	TAOT 1001	None Assigned	0
Patriot State	TAP 1000	None Assigned	0
Patuxent	TAO 201	None Assigned	0
Pecos	TAO 197	None Assigned	0
Peleliu	LHA 5	AP 96624-1620	6
Pennsylvania	SSBN 735	AA 34092-2120	13]
Pensacola	LSD 38	AE 09582-1726	24
Perry, Oliver Hazard	FFG 7	AA 34092-1465	18
Petersburg	TAOT 9101	None Assigned	0
Peterson	DD 969	AE 09582-1207	25
Philadelphia	SSN 690	AE 09582-2370	9
Philip, George	FFG 12	AP 96675-1470	6
Philippine Sea	CG 58	AA 34092-1178	12
Phillips, Franklin J., Pvt	TAK 3004	None Assigned	0
Phoenix	SSN 702	AE 09582-2382	25
Pintado	SSN 672	AP 96675-2352	14
Pioneer	MCM 9	AA 34092-1929	23
Pioneer Commander	TAK 2016	None Assigned	0
Pioneer Contractor	TAK 2018	None Assigned	0
Pioneer Crusader	TAK 2019	None Assigned	0
Pittsburgh	SSN 720	AE 09582-2400	9
Platte	AO 186	AA 34092-3022	25
Pless, Stephen W., Maj.	TAK 3007	None Assigned	0
Pogy	SSN 647	AP 96675-2333	6
Polk, James K.	SSN 645	AA 34092-2072	25
Pollux	TAKR 290	None Assigned	0
Ponce	LPD 15	AE 09582-1717	25
Port Royal	CG 73	AP 96675-1193	14
Portland	LSD 37	AE 09582-1725	24
Portsmouth	SSN 707	AP 96675-2387	6
Potomac	TAOT 181	None Assigned	0
Powhatan	TATF 166	None Assigned	0
Prevail	TAGOS 8	None Assigned	0
Princeton	CG 59	AP 96675-1179	6
Providence	SSN 719	AE 09582-2399	9
Puffer	SSN 652	AP 96675-2338	6

Ship's Name	Hull Number	Zip Code	Home Port
Puget Sound	AD 38	AE 09544-2520	25
Puller, Lewis B.	FFG 23	AP 96675-1479	6
Radford, Arthur W.	DD 968	AE 09586-1206	25
Rainier	AOE 7	AP 96698-3038	27
Ramage	DDG 61	AE 09586-1279	25
Range Sentinel	TAGM 22	None Assigned	0
Ray, David R.	DD 971	AP 96677-1209	4
Regulus	TAKR 292	None Assigned	0
Reid	FFG 30	AP 96677-1486	6
Rentz	FFG 46	AP 96677-1500	6
Rhode Island	SSBN 740	AA 34092-2135	13
Rickover, Hyman G.	SSN 709	AE 09586-2389	25
Rivers, Mendel L.	SSN 636	AA 34092-2366	21
Roberts, Samuel B.	FFG 58	AE 09586-1512	25
Rodgers, John	DD 983	AA 34092-1221	21
Roosevelt, Theodore	DVN 71	AE 09599-2871	25
Rushmore	LSD 47	AP 96677-1735	6
Russell	DDG 59	AP 96677-1257	14
Sacramento	AOE 1	AP 96678-3012	27
Safeguard	ARS 50	AP 96678-3221	14
Saipan	LHA 2	AE 09549-1605	25
Salt Lake City	SSN 716	AP 96678-2396	6
Salvor	ARS 52	AP 96678-3222	14
San Diego	TAFS 6	None Assigned	0
San Francisco	SSN 711	AP 96678-2391	14
San Jacinto	CG 56	AE 09587-1176	25
San Jose	TAFS 7	None Assigned	0
San Juan	SSN 751	AE 09587-2407	9
Sand Lance	SSN 660	AE 09587-2340	21
Santa Barbara	AE 28	AA 34093-3006	21
Santa Fe	SSN 763	AE 09587-2419	9
Saturn	TAFS 10	None Assigned	0
Scan	TAK 5018	None Assigned	0
Scott	DDG 995	AE 09587-1267	25
Scout	MCM 8	AA 34093-1928	23
Scranton	SSN 756	AE 09687-2412	25
Seattle	AOE 3	AE 09587-3014	17
Sentry	MCM 3	AA 34093-1923	23
Shasta	AE 33	AP 96678-3009	3

Ship's Name	Hull Number	Zip Code	Home Port
Shenandoah	AD 44	AE 09551-2540	25
Shiloh	CG 67	AP 96678-1187	6
Shreveport	LPD 12	AE 09587-1714	25
Sides	FFG 14	AP 96678-1472	6
Simon Lake	AS 33	AE 09536-2590	31
Simpson	FFG 56	AE 09587-1510	25
Sioux	TATF 171	None Assigned	0
Sirius	TAFS 8	None Assigned	0
Sirocco	PC 6	AE 09587-1965	24
South Carolina	CGN 37	AE 09587-1164	25
Spadefish	SSN 668	AE 09587-2348	25
Spear, L. Y.	AS 36	AE 09547-2600	25
Spica	TAFS 9	None Assigned	0
Springfield	SSN 761	AE 09587-2417	9
Spruance	DD 963	AA 34093-1201	12
Squall	PC 7	AP 96678-1966	6
Stalwart	TAGOS 1	None Assigned	0
Stark	FFG 31	AA 34093-1487	12
Stethem	DDG 63	None Assigned	0
Stout	DDG 55	AE 09587-1273	25
Strong Texan	TAKR 9670	None Assigned	0
Strong Virginian	TAKR 9205	None Assigned	0
Stuart, Jeb	TAK 9204	None Assigned	0
Stump	DD 978	AE 09587-1216	25
Sumner	TAGS 61	None Assigned	0
Sunfish	SSN 649	AE 09587-2430	25
Supply	AOE 6	AE 09587-3037	25
Tarawa	LHA 1	AP 96622-1600	6
Tautog	SSN 639	AP 96679-2331	14
Taylor	FFG 50	AA 34093-1504	12
Tempest	PC 2	AE 09588-1961	24
Tennessee	SSBN 734	AA 34093-2117	13
Thach	FFG 43	AP 96679-1498	33
Thorn	DD 988	AA 34093-1226	25
Thunderbolt	PC 12	None Assigned	0
Ticonderoga	CG 47	AE 09588-1158	25
Tippecanoe	TAO 199	None Assigned	0
Tisdale, Mahlon S.	FFG 27	AP 96679-1483	6
Titus, Calvin P., Lt. Col.	TAK 5089	None Assigned	0

Ship's Name	Hull Number	Zip Code	Home Port
Toledo	SSN 769	AE 09588-2425	25
Topeka	SSN 754	AP 96679-2410	6
Tortuga	LSD 46	AE 09588-1734	24
Trenton	LPD 14	AE 09588-1716	25
Trepang	SSN 674	AE 09588-2354	9
Tripoli	LPH 10	AP 96626-1645	6
Tucson	SSN 770	None Assigned	0
Tunny	SSN 682	AP 96679-2362	14
Typhoon	PC 5	AE 09588-1964	24
Underwood	FFG 36	AA 34093-1491	12
Valiant	TAOT 94A	None Assigned	0
Valley Forge	CG 50	AP 96682-1170	6
Vandergrift	FFG 48	AP 96682-1502	6
Vanguard	TAG 194	None Assigned	0
Vella Gulf	CG 72	AE 09590-1192	25
Vicksburg	CG 69	AA 34093-1189	12
Victorious	TAGOS 19	None Assigned	0
Vincennes	CG 49	AP 96682-1169	6
Vinson, Carl	CVN 70	AP 96629-2840	2
Wadsworth	FFG 9	AP 96683-1467	6
Warrior	MCM 10	AA 34093-1930	23
Washington, George	CVN 73	AE 09550-2873	25
Wasp	LHD 1	AE 09556-1660	25
Waters	TAGS 45	None Assigned	0
West Virginia	SSBN 736	AA 34093-2123	13
Whidbey Island	LSD 41	AE 09591-1729	24
Wilbur, Curtis	DDG 54	AP 96683-1272	6
Willamette	AO 180	AP 96683-3021	14
Williams, Dewayne T., Pfc	TAK 3009	None Assigned	0
Williams, Jack	FFG 24	AA 34093-2480	12
Wright	TAVB 3	None Assigned	0
Wyman	TAGS 34	None Assigned	0
Yellowstone	AD 41	AE 09512-2525	25
Yorktown	CG 48	AE 09594-1159	25
Young, John	DD 573	AP 96686-1211	6
Yukon	TAO 202	None Assigned	0
Zephyr	PC 8	AP 96687-1967	35
Zeus	TARC 7	None Assigned	0

Chapter 3

LOCATING RESERVE AND NATIONAL GUARD

The Armed Forces Locators (see Chapter Two) will provide the unit of assignment or forward a letter to members of the reserve and National Guard. Members assigned to the inactive reserve and Individual Ready Reserve (IRR) are not assigned to a unit and the locators will only forward a letter to the member's home address (see Chapter Two for procedure).

The Air Force Reserve and Air National Guard

The Air Force locator will forward only one letter per request and will not provide overseas unit of assignment of active members, reserve or Air National Guard units on active duty. Requests for more than one address per letter will be returned without action. Include a self-addressed stamped envelope with request for unit assignment. If the individual is separated from the Air Force you will be so informed.

U.S. Air Force World-Wide Locator
AFPC-MSIMDL
550 C. Street West, Suite 50
Randolph AFB, TX 78150-4752
(210) 652-5775, (210) 652-5774 Recording
($3.50 fee)

The Civil Air Patrol

The Civil Air Patrol is an official auxiliary organization of the U.S. Air Force. Its members are civilian but many are former and retired military. The uniform and insignias of rank are similar to the Air Force. Send inquires to:

Civil Air Patrol (MSPM)
105 S. Hansell Street
Maxwell AFB, AL 36112-6332
(334) 953-6986

The Army Reserve and Inactive Reserve

Army Reserve Personnel Center
ATTN: DARP-VSE
9700 Page Blvd.
St. Louis, MO 63132-5100
(no fee)

The Army National Guard

To locate members of the Army National Guard you must write to the appropriate state Adjutant General (senior military officer of the National Guard in each state). Telephone numbers listed are for military personnel offices (MILPO). There is no research fee.

The State Adjutants General

ALABAMA
Adjutant General
PO Box 3711
Montgomery, AL 36109-0711
(334) 271-7259

ALASKA
Adjutant General
PO Box 5800
Ft. Richardson, AK 99505-5800
(907) 428-6400

ARIZONA
Adjutant General
5636 E. McDowell Road
Phoenix, AZ 65008-3495
(802) 267-2733

ARKANSAS
Adjutant General
Camp Robinson
N. Little Rock, AR 72118
(501) 791-4001

CALIFORNIA
Adjutant General
PO Box 269101
Sacramento, CA 95826-9101
(916) 854-3206

COLORADO
Adjutant General
6848 S. Revere Parkway
Englewood, CO 80112-6710
(303) 397-3173

HAWAII
Adjutant General
3949 Diamond Head Road
Honolulu, HI 96818-4495
(808) 734-2195

IDAHO
Adjutant General
PO Box 45
Boise, ID 83707-0045
(208) 389-5242

ILLINOIS
Adjutant General
1301 N. MacArthur Blvd.
Springfield, IL 62702-2398
(217) 785-3558

INDIANA
Adjutant General
2002 S. Holt Road
Indianapolis, IN 46241-4839
(317) 247-3219

IOWA
Adjutant General
7700 N.W. Beaver Drive
Johnston, IA 50131-1902
(515) 252-4360

KANSAS
Adjutant General
2800 S.W. Topeka Blvd.
Topeka, KS 66611-1287
(913) 274-1061

KENTUCKY
Adjutant General
Boone National Guard Center
Frankfort, KY 40601-6168
(502) 564-8446

LOUISIANA
Adjutant General
Hq Bldg Jackson Barracks
New Orleans, LA 70146-0330
(504) 278-6311

MAINE
Adjutant General
Camp Keyes
Augusta, ME 04333-0033
(207) 626-4571

MASSACHUSETTS
Adjutant General
25 Haverhill Rd Camp Guild
Reading, MA 01667-1999
(617) 944-0500

MINNESOTA
Adjutant General
20 W. 12th Street
St Paul, MN 56155
(612) 282-4040

MISSOURI
Adjutant General
1717 Industrial Drive
Jefferson City, MO 85101
(314) 526-9648

NEBRASKA
Adjutant General
1300 Military Road
Lincoln, NE 68508-1090
(402) 471-7115

NEW HAMPSHIRE
Adjutant General
#1 Airport Road
Concord, NH 03301-5353
(603) 225-1205

NEW MEXICO
Adjutant General
PO Box 4277
Santa Fe, NM 87502-4277
(505) 474-1253

MARYLAND
Adjutant General
5th Regiment Armory
Baltimore, MD 21201-2266
(410) 576-6011

MICHIGAN
Adjutant General
2500 S. Washington Avenue
Lansing, MI 48913-5101
(517) 483-5514

MISSISSIPPI
Adjutant General
PO Box 5027
Jackson, MS 39296-5027
(601) 973-6324

MONTANA
Adjutant General
PO Box 4789
Helena, MT 59604-4788
(406) 444-6925

NEVADA
Adjutant General
2525 S. Carson Street
Carson City, NV 89701-5502
(702) 887-7258

NEW JERSEY
Adjutant General
Eggert Crossing Road, Cn 340
Trenton, NJ 08625-0340
(609) 562-0652

NEW YORK
Adjutant General
330 Old Niskayuna Road
Latham, NY 12110-2224
(518) 786-4570

NORTH CAROLINA
Adjutant General
4105 Reedy Creek Road
Raleigh, NC 27607-6410
(919) 664-6120

OHIO
Adjutant General
2825 W. Granville Road
Columbus, OH 43235-2712
(614) 889-7040

OREGON
Adjutant General
1776 Militia Way N.E.
Salem, OR 97309-5047
(503) 945-3939

PUERTO RICO
Adjutant General
PO Box 3786
San Juan, PR 00904-3786
(809) 724-1500

SOUTH CAROLINA
Adjutant General
1 National Guard Road
Columbia, SC 28201-3117
(803) 748-4228

TENNESSEE
Adjutant General
PO Box 41502
Nashville, TN 37204-1501
(615) 532-3106

UTAH
Adjutant General
PO Box 1776
Draper, UT 84020-1776
(801) 576-3616

NORTH DAKOTA
Adjutant General
PO Box 5511, Fraine Bks
Bismarck, ND 58502-5511
(701) 224-592

OKLAHOMA
Adjutant General
3501 Military Circle N.E.
Oklahoma City, OK 73111
(405) 425-8203

PENNSYLVANIA
Adjutant General
Dept of Military Affairs
Annville, PA 17003-5002
(717) 861-8531

RHODE ISLAND
Adjutant General
1051 N. Main Street
Providence, RI 02904-5717
(401) 457-4135

SOUTH DAKOTA
Adjutant General
2823 W. Main Street
Rapid City, SD 57702-8186
(605) 399-6710

TEXAS
Adjutant General
PO Box 5218
Austin, TX 78763-5218
(512) 465-5031

VERMONT
Adjutant General
Bldg #1, Camp Johnson
Colchester, VT 05446
(802) 654-0130

VIRGINIA
Adjutant General
501 E. Franklin Street
Richmond, VA 23218-2317
(804) 775-9116

VIRGIN ISLANDS
Adjutant General
Alexander Hamilton Airport
St. Croix, VI 00850-2380
(808) 772-7732

WASHINGTON
Adjutant General
Camp Murray
Tacoma, WA 98430-5000
(206) 512-8248

WEST VIRGINIA
Adjutant General
1703 Coonskin Drive
Charleston, WV 25311-1085
(304) 341-6404

WISCONSIN
Adjutant General
3020 Wright Street
Madison, WI 53708-6111
(608) 242-3444

WYOMING
Adjutant General
PO Box 1709
Cheyenne, WY 62003-1709
(307) 772-5203

State Guard

Several states have State Guard or Defense Organizations which are not a part of the National Guard but are volunteer military units that come under the jurisdiction of the State Adjutant General. Contact each state Adjutant General separately for information on their members. (See above list for addresses.) No research fee.

The following states have State Guards:

Alaska	Alabama
Arizona	California
Colorado	Florida
Georgia	Illinois
Indiana	Louisiana
Massachusetts	Maryland
Montana	Michigan
Mississippi	North Carolina
New Hampshire	New Mexico

Nevada	New York
Ohio	Oklahoma
Oregon	Pennsylvania
Puerto Rico	Rhode Island
South Carolina	Tennessee
Texas	Utah
Virginia	Vermont
Washington	West Virginia

For additional information, contact:

State Defense Force Association of U.S.
213 Congress, Suite 339
Austin, Texas 78701
(512) 266-2350

The Coast Guard Reserve

The Coast Guard will provide assignment and unit telephone numbers of reserve personnel when requested by telephone.

Commandant
U.S. Coast Guard
2100 2nd Street, S.W.
Washington, DC 20593-0001
(202) 267-0547, (202) 267-4553 Fax
($3.50 fee)

The Coast Guard Auxiliary

The U.S. Coast Guard Auxiliary, which has 40,000 members, is a non-military organization created by Congress to assist the Coast Guard to promote boating efficiency and safety. Members of this organization wear uniforms and insignias similar to the Coast Guard. For additional information, contact:

U.S. Coast Guard
2100 Second Street, S.W.
Washington, DC 20593-0001
(202) 267-1077, (202) 267-4460 Fax

The Marine Corps Selected Reserve

U.S. Marine Corps - CMC
Marine Corps (MMSB-10)
2008 Elliot Road, Room 201
Quantico, VA 22134-5030
(703) 784-3942
($3.50 fee)

Marine Corps Individual Ready Reserve, Fleet Marine Corps Reserve or Inactive Reserve

Marine Corps Reserve Support Center
10950 El Monte
Overland Park, KS 66211-1408
(913) 491-7502
(no fee)

The Navy Active Reserve

Bureau of Naval Personnel
PERS-324
2 Navy Annex
Washington, DC 20370-3240
(703) 614-5011, (703) 614-3155 Recording
(703) 614-1261 Fax
($3.50 fee)

The Navy Individual Ready Reserve (IRR) and Inactive Reserve

Personnel Locator Service
4400 Dauphin Street
New Orleans, LA 70149-7800
(800) 535-2699
($3.50 fee)

They will forward a letter only; they do not provide addresses. Do not put a return address on the letter to be forwarded.

Locating Reserve and National Guard through the Department of Veterans Affairs

Members of the reserves and National Guard who have served on active duty in the armed forces are considered veterans and may have applied for veterans benefits. Numerous members of the reserve components are eligible for educational benefits under the Montgomery Act which is administered by the Department of Veterans Affairs (VA). These individuals may also be contacted through the VA (see Chapter Five for details).

Chapter 4

LOCATING RETIRED MILITARY

This chapter describes methods of locating retired military members using the Armed Forces World-Wide Locators and the retired pay centers.

The Armed Forces World-Wide Locators will forward letters to *retired members* of the armed forces. (See Chapter Two for details.) These include those who have retired from active duty, the reserve or National Guard. Reserve and National Guard members do not become eligible for retired pay until age 60 and are usually members of the inactive reserve until that time. Inactive reserve may be located through the reserve (see Chapter Three) or the Department of Veterans Affairs (see Chapter Five).

Air Force: Retired from Active Duty, Reserve, or National Guard

The Air Force locator will forward only one letter per request. Requests for more than one address per letter will be returned without action.

U.S. Air Force World-Wide Locator
AFPC-MSIMDL
550 C. Street West, Suite 50
Randolph AFB, TX 78150-4752
(210) 652-5775, (210) 652-5774 Recording
http://www.afpc.af.mil
($3.50 fee)

Army: Retired from Active Duty, Reserve or National Guard

Army Reserve Personnel Center
IMP-F
9700 Page Blvd
St. Louis, MO 63132-5200
(314) 538-3798
http://www.army.mil/retire-p/locat.htm
(No fee)

Coast Guard: Retired from Active Duty or Reserve

Commanding Officer (RAS)
U.S. Coast Guard Pay and Personnel Center
444 S.E. Quincy Street
Topeka, KS 66683-3591
(913) 357-3415, (913) 295-2639 Fax
(No fee)

Marine Corps: Retired from Active Duty or Reserve

CMC (MMSR-6)
HQ Marine Corps
2 Navy Annex
Washington, DC 20380-1775
(703) 614-1901, (703) 614-4400 Fax, (No Fee)

Navy: Retired from Active Duty or Reserve

Commanding Officer
Naval Reserve Personnel Center
4400 Dauphine Street
New Orleans, LA 70149-7800
(504) 678-5400, (504) 678-6934 Fax
(800) 535-2699
($3.50 fee)
http://www.navy.mil/navpalib/people/faq/.www/locatehtml
(Do not put a return address on letter to be forwarded.)

RETIRED FROM OTHER UNIFORMED SERVICES:

National Oceanic and Atmospheric Administration

Department of Commerce
Commissioned Personnel Center, NOAA
1315 E-West Highway, Room 12100
Silver Spring, MD 20910-3282
(301) 713-3453, (301) 713-4140 Fax
(800) 224-NOAA
(No fee)

U.S. Public Health Service Personnel

U.S. Public Health Service
330 Independence Avenue, S.W.
Room 1040
Washington, DC 20201
(800) 638-8744, (202) 619-1851 Fax

Locating Retired Military through Defense Finance and Accounting Services

If a locator is unable to identify the person you are looking for, contact the appropriate Defense Finance and Accounting Office. You may be able to get some assistance from them. Their phone numbers are listed below. These centers maintain files of all retired military members (active duty, reserve and National Guard) and Survivor Benefit Plan annuitants (widows, widowers and some dependent children). They can reveal to third parties the names and rank/rate of retired members and annuitants. They can also forward letters to the retired members and annuitants in a similar manner as regular locators. The SSN of the retiree is usually required. There is no fee for this service.

- Army, Air Force, Navy and Marine Corps retired pay accounts: (800) 321-1080, (800) 469-6559 Fax
- Army, Air Force, Navy and Marine Corps Survivors Benefits annuitants: (800) 435-3396
- Coast Guard and National Oceanic Atmospheric Administration: (800) 772-8724

Locating Widows/Widowers of Military Retirees

It may be possible to have a letter forwarded to a widow or widower of an individual who retired from the armed forces (active duty, reserve or National Guard). If the widow or widower is receiving survivor's benefits from a particular service, the benefactor's address may be contained in the files of the appropriate finance center. However, note that not all spouses receive these benefits. The Privacy Act prohibits releasing their address, but the service may forward a letter as they will for retirees. For more information, contact the appropriate finance center. (The telephone numbers are listed in the preceding section.) SSN of the sponsor may be required. Spouses and dependent children may also be located through the VA in many cases.

Retirement Services Officers

Most major military installations have retirement service officers or retiree activity officers who assist retirees by providing information on retired benefits and services. These officers deal closely with the retired military population and may be able to provide some assistance in locating retired members in their service areas. Call the base or post information operator for their telephone number (see Chapter Two).

How to Determine the Social Security Number of a Retired Officer

The Social Security numbers of many retired officers and warrant officers may be obtained from the Officer's Registers. See the Library section of Chapter Eight for complete details.

Chapter 5

LOCATING VETERANS

For the purpose of this book the word "veteran" means a person who served on active duty in one or more of the armed forces.

This chapter explains how to locate veterans of the armed forces and former members of the reserve and National Guard using:

- *Department of Veterans Affairs (VA)*
- *National Personnel Records Center*
- *Veterans organizations*
- *Military reunion organizations*
- *Private organizations*

Department of Veterans Affairs

The Department of Veterans Affairs (formerly the Veterans Administration) is very cooperative in providing assistance in locating veterans. There are over 26 million living veterans. Approximately 80,000 are veterans of World War I, nine million are veterans of World War II, five million are veterans of the Korean War and eight million are veterans of the war in Vietnam. The remaining five million are peace time veterans.

The VA does not have addresses of all veterans listed in their files. It lists addresses only of those individuals who have at some time applied for VA benefits, such as educational assistance, medical care, disability compensation, pensions, home loans, and VA insurance. The address in their files is the address given when the veteran last obtained or applied for VA benefits. Since 1974 the VA has the name and SSN of all individuals who are discharged from all branches of the armed forces, but do not have an address unless the individual makes a claim.

The VA will forward a letter in a similar manner as the armed forces (see Chapter Two). Before attempting to have a letter forwarded, it is recommended that you first call the VA. By dialing (800) 827-1000, you will automatically be connected with the VA Regional Office closest to you. They will not give you an address over the phone, but explain to the VA counselor that you wish to verify that a veteran is listed in their files and that they have a current address before you mail any correspondence to be forwarded. Give the individual's full name and service number, social security number or VA file or claim number, if known. If you do not have this information the VA can sometimes identify veterans with either their date of birth, city and state that the person entered the service, branch of service, middle name or possibly the name alone, if the person has a unique name. If the individual is listed in the files, ask for their VA claim number.

If the Regional Office cannot find the individual in their file, then contact the VA Insurance Office.

Department of Veterans Affairs
PO Box 8079
Philadelphia, PA 19101
(800) 669-8477

For veterans who have been separated for less than five years, contact:

Servicemen Group Life Insurance
213 Washington Street
Newark, NJ 07102-2999
(800) 419–1473
(201) 802-7676 (from overseas call collect)

These offices have insurance information in their files that is not readily available in the regional offices' files.

To forward a letter, place your correspondence in an unsealed, stamped envelope without your return address. Put the veteran's name and VA claim number on the front of the envelope. Next prepare a short fact sheet and state that you request that the VA forward this letter to the veteran. Tell them you were given the VA claim number by their Regional Office. Also include all other pertinent information to ensure they can identify the veteran. Include as much information as you can such as name, service number, SSN, date of birth, city and state entered service, etc. Next, place this letter and the fact sheet in a larger envelope and mail to the VA Regional Office you spoke with or where that office instructed you to send it. If they cannot identify the individual, they will return your letter to you. They will also inform you if the letter is undeliverable by the Post Office.

You may contact any VA Regional Office by dialing (800) 827-1000. You will be automatically connected with the VA Regional Office closest to you. You may also contact the appropriate VA Regional Office by using the directory at the end of this chapter. The local numbers are being phased out in the near future. If there is no number listed, you can only contact that office using the 800 number.

Obtaining Information from the VA by Telephone

There is a great deal of identifying information you may be able to obtain from the Department of Veterans Affairs (VA) over the telephone. Call any VA Regional Office and tell them you want to forward a letter to a veteran if they have his address on file (even if this is not your intent). Explain that there is no reason for you to send the letter if they do not have an address. Ask if they can identify the veteran from the information you have. See previous section for details.

If the VA Regional Office can identify the veteran, you may be able to obtain some of the following information: service number, date of birth, VA claim number, if the veteran went to college on the GI bill, the name of the college he attended and the dates attended. The VA is required to tell you the location of the veteran's file, whether it is in a Regional Office or in a records holding area.

If the address is not over three or four years old, the veteran is probably living within 300 miles of the VA Regional Office where the file is located. Check with telephone information operators in cities within this radius. If you do a computer surname search with the Nationwide Locator (see Appendix B) against the National Telephone Directory file, you will most likely get a current address. If you are able to obtain a date of birth, then you can do a driver license or date of birth computer search. With the veteran's service number, you may be able to obtain a copy of the military records under the Freedom of Information Act. The record has the veteran's date of birth, place of entry and separation from the service and other valuable information. With either a service number or a date of birth, you can in some cases obtain a Social Security number (see next section).

If the VA counselor you are dealing with is not cooperative and tells you they cannot give any information because of the Privacy Act, then discontinue your conversation. Call again and you will likely get another counselor who may be more helpful. Be persistent and courteous and you will eventually obtain some important identifying information that will enable you to locate the person you are seeking.

Obtaining a Veteran's SSN through the VA

You may be able to obtain a SSN for a veteran if the veteran applied for benefits after April 1973 and the veteran's name, service number or date of birth is provided. Send a check in the amount of two dollars payable to Department of Veterans Affairs to the address below. State in your letter that you want the veteran's VA Claim number (do not ask for the veterans SSN). If the number returned is nine digits then it is the veteran's SSN. Mail request to:

VA Records Processing Center
PO Box 5020
St. Louis, MO 63115

Mailing from a Roster, Muster Roll or List

The VA Records Processing Center (RPC) is located in St. Louis, Missouri. Do not confuse this office with the National Personnel Records Center (NPRC) which is also located in St Louis. RPC is responsible for research of large groups of veterans. This research will enable people to forward letters for military reunion notifications or to secure statements to substantiate (prove) VA disability claims. RPC can do research from copies of unit rosters, ship's muster rolls and compiled lists that contain names and service numbers. Anyone may use this service whether or not they are a veteran.

There are two ways to obtain information from the VA Records Processing Center. First, you can submit a list of veteran's names and service numbers (see section on unit and ship rosters in Chapter Eight). You may also submit any of the following if you do not have a service number to help identify the veteran:

- Social Security number
- VA file or claim number
- Date of birth
- Place of entry into service (city and state)
- Name only (if veteran has a unique name)
- Branch of service

Include a check or money order for $2.00 for each name to be researched, payable to the Department of Veterans Affairs (personal checks are acceptable). The center will research the names and provide the following information:

- VA file or claim number
- VA folder location (VA Regional Office)
- That the veteran is deceased and date of death, if known.
- If the VA does not have a record, they will notify you of this. (Probably the veteran has never applied for VA benefits.)
- That they cannot identify the veteran from the information provided.

The information will be returned to you along with instructions on how to have letters forwarded to the veterans. Submit the letters with the VA claim number and name on an unsealed envelope, use sufficient postage to cover mailing costs and do not use a return address. Letters involving debt collections will not be forwarded.

The VA cannot assure that the veteran will either receive or respond to this correspondence. If the letter is returned to the VA by the Post Office as undeliverable, the inquirer will be notified approximately five weeks after the letter is mailed.

The VA file number is sometimes referred to as the VA claim number and, in some cases, may be the same as the veteran's Social Security number. Since June 1974, the VA has used Social Security numbers as VA Claim numbers. Claim numbers in this category will have the letter "C" (XC if deceased) followed by the nine digit SSN without any dashes or spaces.

The second way to use this center's service is to send the letters, names and payments together. The center will do the necessary research and forward the letters. This process usually takes up to two weeks to complete; however, in peak periods it may take four to six weeks. Send rosters and payment or rosters, letters and payment to:

VA Records Processing Center
PO Box 5020
St. Louis, MO 63115
(314) 263-2597

The National Personnel Records Center

The National Personnel Records Center (NPRC) will forward correspondence to a veteran's last known address which is usually the one given when the individual separated from active duty or when a reserve commitment was completed. This is done only in limited situations which include:

- Requester's VA or Social Security benefits are dependent on contacting the veteran.
- Veteran to be contacted will have veterans benefits affected.
- Forwarding is in veteran's/next of kin's interest e.g., estate settlement.
- Veterans who may have fathered children.
- Financial institution's legitimate effort to collect a debt.

A search fee of $3.50 is applicable only when the forwarding of correspondence is not in the veteran's interest, e.g., debt collection. Make checks payable to "Treasurer of the U.S."

The NPRC will place the letter to be forwarded in another envelope and will add the individual's name and last known address. In the event the letter is not delivered, it will be returned to the NPRC and you will not be informed.

If a person writes to the NPRC for assistance in locating a veteran and the reason does not fall into any of the above categories, the writer will be informed to contact the nearest VA Regional Office (for requests of fewer than five names) or the VA Records Processing Center (for requests of five or more names). Requests should have the name, SSN, service number or VA claim number. See preceding sections for details.

National Personnel Records Center
9700 Page Blvd
St. Louis, MO 63132

In July 1973 a fire at the NPRC destroyed about 80% of the records for Army personnel discharged between November 1, 1912 and January 1, 1960. About 75% of the records for Air Force personnel with surnames from Hubbard through "Z" who were discharged between September 25, 1947 and January 1, 1964 were also destroyed. Some alternative information may be obtained from records of the state Adjutants General (see Chapter Three) and state Veterans Service offices. There are currently over 50 million military records at the NPRC.

Locating Former Members of the U.S. Coast Guard

In addition to the information provided in previous chapters, the Coast Guard will forward letters to veterans of the Coast Guard at their last known address. There is a $3.50 fee. Send letters to:

Commandant
CGPC-ADM-3
2100 2nd Street, S.W.
Washington, DC 20593-0001
(202) 267-1340, (202) 267-4985 Fax

For Internet users, Fred's Place is a web site dedicated to Coast Guard information and addresses of Coast Guard veterans. The address is: http://www.cris.com/~fsiegel.

Selective Service Records

The classification records of men who were registered for the draft under the Selective Service Act and information from ledger books are available to the public. These classification records list name, date of birth, draft classification, date to report for induction and in some cases date of separation. Records were maintained from 1940 to 1975. These records are maintained at various federal record centers (by state and county). All requests for information must be made through:

National Headquarters
Selective Service System
1550 Wilson Blvd., Suite 400
Arlington, VA 22209-2426
(703) 235-2555, (703) 235-2212 Fax

Locating Current and Former Merchant Mariners

The Merchant Marines is a civil organization and refers to the nation's commercial shipping industry. It is not an armed or uniformed service of the United States. However, many merchant mariners and officers are members of the Navy, Coast Guard, and Army reserves. You may locate them through the appropriate military reserve (see Chapter Three). Graduates of the U.S. Merchant Marine Academy at Kings Point, New York, are appointed officers in the U.S. Navy reserve. The U.S. Coast Guard registers all merchant seamen and will forward a letter to the last known address of the mariner. There is no charge for this service. The letter must be placed in an envelope with a stamp and no return address and mailed to:

Commandant
CGPC-ADM-3
2100 Second Street, S.W.
Washington, DC 20593-0001
(202) 267-1340, (202) 267-4985 Fax
($3.50) fee

Contact the following organizations, if searching for a merchant marine.

U.S. Merchant Marine Veterans of World War II
PO Box 629
San Pedro, CA 90733
(310) 519-9545, (310) 519-0265 Fax
This organization will list your search in their publication.

American Merchant Marine Veterans
4720 S.E. 15th Avenue, Suite 202
Cape Coral, FL 33904-9600
(941) 549-1010, (941) 549-1990 Fax

In January 1988, a federal court decision awarded veteran status to all merchant seamen who served in World War II (December 7, 1941 to August 15, 1945).

You may attempt to contact members of this group through the Department of Veterans Affairs.

Veterans, Military, and Patriotic Organizations

Veterans, military, and patriotic organizations can help in locating veterans and in providing information about military reunions. The service and assistance vary with each organization. Most have magazines or newsletters that publish names of veterans that people are trying to locate and dates that military unit reunions are being held.

The addresses and telephone numbers of most national organizations are listed at the end of this chapter. When contacting an organization, list as much information as is known such as: names, aliases, nicknames, date of birth, dates of service, rank, service or SSN (see sample letter on page 123). Usually there are no fees required for these services. The associations will normally forward a letter.

Locating Former Air Force and Army Air Force Pilot Cadets

The Aviation Cadet Alumni Association was formed as a no-dues, non-profit organization. It tries to provide ex-cadets with current addresses of their former classmates. Former Air Force and Army Air Force Cadets are invited to submit their flying class, primary, basic and advanced schools. The association currently has approximately 30,000 names and addresses of former pilots representing classes from 1922 to 1962 (with a few later ones). Searches for individuals will not be attempted. Printouts of classes are available to participants who send their flight class, primary, basic and advanced schools along with a self-addressed stamped envelope to the address below:

Robert C. White
54 Seton Trail
Ormond Beach, FL 32176

Army Quartermaster Roll Call

The Army Quartermaster Roll Call preserves veteran's names, places of birth, dates of service, units of assignment and highest ranks or grades held. It is recorded in the U.S. Army Quartermaster Museum at Fort Lee, VA, home of the Quartermaster Corps. For more information, write to:

The Army Quartermaster Roll Call
PO Box A
Fort Lee, VA 23801

The American War Library

The American War Library has established an extensive database of information concerning American wars and a locator database of over eight million veterans and personnel on active duty. There is a small fee. This database may provide an address of a current or former military member.

The American War Library
16907 Brighton Avenue, Suite D
Gardena, CA 90247
(310) 530-0177, (310) 532-0634 Fax
E-Mail: amerwar@aol.com
http://home.earthlink.net/~amerwar

Locating Former Military Doctors

There are two medical directories that list the names and current addresses of physicians. These are recommended to disabled veterans who are trying to substantiate a medical claim and need to locate the physicians who treated them for their service-connected disabilities. They are *The Directory of Medical Specialists* by Marquis Who's Who, and *The American Medical Directory* by the American Medical Association.

Both references list a doctor's medical specialty and type of practice. The *Directory of Medical Specialists* also provides biographical information, such as military service, including a physician's service period, branch of military service, and former rank.

This biographical information can be particularly helpful to disabled veterans who cannot remember their doctor's first name. Both directories can usually be found in large public libraries. Another source that disabled veterans might find useful in locating physicians is the American Medical Association's computer datafile in Chicago. Veterans can request the address of a physician by writing to:

Data Release
American Medical Association
515 N. State Street
Chicago, IL 60610
(312) 464-5199

Locating Veterans to Substantiate VA Claims

To substantiate claims for disability through the VA, you may need to locate other veterans you served with to obtain statements concerning injuries and wounds. You should do the following:

Obtain the assistance of a Veteran Service Officer of an accredited national veterans organization (e.g., The American Legion, VFW, Disabled American Veterans, AMVETS, etc.). They can help obtain rosters from the National Personnel Records Center, the Archives or the appropriate military service. They will also obtain assistance for you from the Department of Veterans Affairs. There is no fee for these services nor do you need to be a member of the organization. See your local telephone book for the listings of these organizations.

Obtain copies from the National Personnel Records Center of your entire military personnel and medical records and rosters of the unit in which you served when the disability occurred. Do not mention "VA claim" on your request for medical records. (See Chapter Eight.)

Prepare letters to all the veterans listed on the rosters and send letters to the VA Records Processing Center for forwarding. Even if some of the individuals were unaware of the event, they may know the addresses of other former members of the unit.

To locate officers and warrant officers, obtain service number, date of birth or Social Security number from appropriate officer's register. Have The Nationwide Locator (see Appendix B) do Social Security traces for all Social Security numbers located. For officers with service numbers, forward letters through the VA or have The Nationwide Locator do driver's license or a date of birth search.

For those veterans the VA does not have an address for, search National Telephone Directories available on CD-ROM and on the Internet.

To determine if your unit has a reunion group, check with all reunion registries listed at the end of this chapter. If a reunion group is located, ask for the addresses of individuals desired or ask that your letters be forwarded to them.

Publish "need-to-find" notices in all appropriate veterans organization magazines and newsletters. (See "Newspapers and Magazines," Chapter Thirteen.) Send letters to all appropriate veterans organizations and request that they check their membership for the veterans you are seeking. Request that they provide you with the addresses or forward your letter.

Obtain dates of birth of remaining veterans from the VA or from individual military records from the National Personnel Record Center and do driver license and date of birth searches. (See Chapters Eight and Appendix B.)

For the remaining veterans that are not located, contact local veterans organizations, mayors, newspapers, police chiefs, postmasters, high schools and churches in their home town, if known. (See Chapter Thirteen).

Send letters to the Social Security Administration and the Internal Revenue Service for forwarding. (See Chapter Thirteen.)

Searching for Birth Parents

Locating a birth parent (for someone who was placed for adoption) may seem like an impossible task. This is not always true. Numerous birth parents who were in the military have been located with the use of the information in this book.

In every search it is extremely important to gather as much information as possible. In searches for birth parents, it is vital to gather every scrap of so-called relevant and irrelevant information. This information must be obtained from adoption agencies, hospitals, doctors, attorneys, friends, family, neighbors and anyone who may have any information concerning the birth parents. Sometimes a small bit of information may be the very thing it takes to solve a case. Records must be searched as well as newspaper files. Try to find old letters, photographs, phone and address books, medical information, etc. This information is especially valuable if the birth parent (or a realtive of the birth parent) was ever in the military.

The military has records on everyone who is or was in the service. Individual military records show when and where an individual was assigned, as well as other identifying information. Most of these records still exist and are located in the National Personnel Records Center, the Department of Veterans Affairs, military and civilian libraries, historical organizations and military reunion organizations. These records consist of unit rosters, muster rolls of ships' members, officers' registers, morning reports, ships' logs, troop lists, unit year books, photographs, lists of old Army and Air Force Post Offices as well as Fleet Post Offices, etc. All of these are excellent sources of information. There are also military records that list where units were stationed, ship home ports, and where the ships traveled.

There is a special office in the National Personnel Records Center that will assist individuals who are searching for a birth parent if a name, location or unit is known. They will search organizational and individual records to obtain service numbers, dates of birth and last known address. For assistance, write:

Director
National Personnel Records Center
9700 Page Blvd
St. Louis, MO 63132

Birth parents have been located with such sketchy information as just a first or a last name. In other cases, birth parents have been located without a name, but with a unit, a ship, a military base, a picture, rank, military job, old letters, names of friends, etc. Birth parents with common names like Joe Smith have been located in a relatively short period of time.

Each birth parent search is different and, as a result, there is no set pattern or course on how to proceed on any particular search. Persistence is the most important factor. There is always information, but it may take many attempts to obtain it. Never give up! If you persevere you will ultimately find the person you are seeking.

Directory of VA Regional Offices

ALABAMA
VA Regional Office
345 Perry Hill Road
Montgomery, AL 36109
(334) 279-4866

ALASKA
VA Regional Office
2925 DeBarr Road
Anchorage, AK 99508-2989
(907) 257-4700

ARIZONA
VA Regional Office
3225 N. Central Avenue
Phoenix, AZ 85012
(602) 263-5411

ARKANSAS
VA Regional Office
Bldg 65, Ft. Roots
N. Little Rock, AR 72115
(501) 370-3800

CALIFORNIA
VA Regional Office
11000 Wilshire Blvd.
Los Angeles, CA 90024
(213) 479-4011

CALIFORNIA
VA Regional Office
2022 Camino Del Rio, N.
San Diego, CA 92108
(619) 297-8220

CALIFORNIA
VA Regional Office
1301 Clay Street
Oakland, CA 94612
(510) 637-1325

COLORADO
VA Regional Office
44 Union Blvd.
Denver, CO 80225
(303) 980-1300

CONNECTICUT
VA Regional Office
450 Main Street
Hartford, CT 06103
(203) 278-3230

DELAWARE
VA Regional Office
1601 Kirkwood Highway
Wilmington, DE 19805
(302) 998-0191

DISTRICT OF COLUMBIA
VA Regional Office
1120 Vermont Ave, N.W.
Washington, DC 20421

FLORIDA
VA Regional Office
144 First Avenue, S.
St Petersburg, FL 33701
(813) 898-2121

GEORGIA
VA Regional Office
730 Peachtree St, N.E.
Atlanta, GA 30365
(404) 881-1776

HAWAII
VA Regional Office
300 Ala Moana Blvd.
Honolulu, HI 96850
(808) 566-1000

IDAHO
VA Regional Office
805 W. Franklin Street
Boise, ID 83702
(208) 334-1010

INDIANA
VA Regional Office
575 N. Pennsylvania St
Indianapolis, IN 46202
(317) 226-5566

KANSAS
VA Regional Office
5500 E. Kellogg
Wichita, KS 67211
(316) 682-2301

LOUISIANA
VA Regional Office
701 Loyola Avenue
New Orleans, LA 70113
(504) 589-7191

MARYLAND
VA Regional Office
31 Hopkins Plaza
Baltimore, MD 21201
(410) 685-5454

MICHIGAN
VA Regional Office
477 Michigan Avenue
Detroit, MI 48226
(313) 964-5110

MISSISSIPPI
VA Regional Office
100 W. Capitol Street
Jackson, MS 39269
(601) 965-4873

ILLINOIS
VA Regional Office
536 S. Clark Street
Chicago, IL 60680
(312) 663-5510

IOWA
VA Regional Office
210 Walnut Street
Des Moines, IA 50309
(515) 284-0219

KENTUCKY
VA Regional Office
545 S. Third Street
Louisville, KY 40202
(502) 584-2231

MAINE
VA Regional Office
Route 17 East
Togus, ME 04330
(207) 623-8000

MASSACHUSETTS
VA Regional Office
JFK Federal Bldg, Govt Ctr
Boston, MA 02203
(617) 227-4600

MINNESOTA
VA Regional Office
Fed Bldg, Ft. Snelling
St Paul, MN 55111
(612) 726-1454

MISSOURI
VA Regional Office
400 South 18th Street
St Louis, MO 63103
(314) 342-1171

MONTANA
VA Regional Office
Williams St & Hwy 12W
Ft Harrison, MT 59636
(406) 447-7975

NEBRASKA
VA Regional Office
5631 S 48th Street
Lincoln, NE 68516
(402) 437-5001

NEVADA
VA Regional Office
1201 Terminal Way
Reno, NV 89520
(702) 329-9244

NEW HAMPSHIRE
VA Regional Office
275 Chestnut Street
Manchester, NH 03101
(603) 666-7785

NEW JERSEY
VA Regional Office
20 Washington Place
Newark, NJ 07102
(201) 645-2150

NEW MEXICO
VA Regional Office
500 Gold Avenue, S.W.
Albuquerque, NM 87102
(505) 766-3361

NEW YORK
VA Regional Office
111 W. Huron Street
Buffalo, NY 14202
(716) 846-5191

NEW YORK
VA Regional Office
245 W. Houston Street
New York City, NY 10014
(212) 807-7229

NORTH CAROLINA
VA Regional Office
251 N. Main Street
Winston-Salem, NC 27155
(919) 748-1800

NORTH DAKOTA
VA Regional Office
2101 Elm Street
Fargo, ND 58102
(701) 293-3656

OHIO
VA Regional Office
1240 E. 9th Street
Cleveland, OH 44199
(216) 621-5050

OKLAHOMA
VA Regional Office
125 S. Main Street
Muskogee, OK 74401
(918) 687-2500

OREGON
VA Regional Office
1220 S.W. 3rd Avenue
Portland, OR 97204
(503) 221-2431

PENNSYLVANIA
VA Regional Office
5000 Wissahickon Avenue
Philadelphia, PA 19101
(215) 438-5225

PENNSYLVANIA
VA Regional Office
1000 Liberty Avenue
Pittsburgh, PA 15222
(412) 281-4233

PUERTO RICO
VA Regional Office
GPO Box 4867
San Juan, PR 00936
(809) 766-5141

SOUTH CAROLINA
VA Regional Office
1801 Assembly Street
Columbia, SC 29201
(803) 765-5861

TENNESSEE
VA Regional Office
110 9th Avenue, South
Nashville, TN 37203
(615) 736-5251

TEXAS
VA Regional Office
1400 N. Valley Mills Drive
Waco, TX 76799
(817) 772-3060

VERMONT
VA Regional Office
N. Hartland Road
White River Jctn, VT 05001
(802) 296-5177

WASHINGTON
VA Regional Office
915 2nd Avenue
Seattle, WA 98174
(206) 624-7200

PHILIPPINES
VA Regional Office
1131 Roxas Blvd.
APO, AP 96440
(810) 521-7521

RHODE ISLAND
VA Regional Office
380 Westminster Mall
Providence, RI 02903
(401) 273-4910

SOUTH DAKOTA
VA Regional Office
2501 W. 22nd Street
Sioux Falls, SD 57117
(605) 336-3496

TEXAS
VA Regional Office
8900 Lakes At 610 Drive
Houston, TX 77054
(713) 664-4664

UTAH
VA Regional Office
125 S. State Street
Salt Lake City, UT 84147
(801) 524-5960

VIRGINIA
VA Regional Office
210 Franklin Road, S.W.
Roanoke, VA 24011
(703) 857-2109

WEST VIRGINIA
VA Regional Office
640 Fourth Avenue
Huntington, WV 25701
(304) 529-5720

WISCONSIN
VA Regional Office
5000 W. National Avenue B-6
Milwaukee, WI 53295
(414) 383-8680

WYOMING
VA Regional Office
2360 E. Pershing Blvd.
Cheyenne, WY 82001
(307) 778-7396

Directory of Military and Patriotic Organizations

Organization

Numbers

Air Force Association
1501 Lee Highway
Arlington, VA 22209-1198
E-mail: mbrserv@afa.org
(180,000 members)

(703) 247-5800
(703) 247-5831 Fax

Air Force Sergeants Association
PO Box 50
Temple Hills, MD 20757
(162,000 members)

(301) 899-3500
(301) 899-8136 Fax

American Ex-Prisoners of War
3201 East Pioneer Parkway #40
Arlington, TX 76010-5396
(33,000 members)

(817) 649-2979
(817) 649-0109 Fax

American GI Forum of the U.S.
206 San Pedro, Suite 200
San Antonio, TX 78205
(143,000 members)

(210) 223-4096
(210) 223-4970 Fax

The American Legion
PO Box 1055
Indianapolis, IN 46206
(3,000,000 members)

(317) 630-1366
(317) 630-1241 Fax

American Military Retirees
  Association, Inc.
426 U.S. Oval, Suite 1200
Plattsburg, NY 12903
(10,000 members)

(518) 563-9479
Phone and Fax

American Retirees Association   (703) 527-3065
2009 N. 14th Street #300   (703) 528-4229 Fax
Arlington, VA 22201-2514
(1,500 members)

American Veterans of WWII   (301) 459-9600
   Korea and Vietnam (AMVETS)   (301) 459-7924 Fax
4647 Forbes Boulevard
Lanham, MD 20706
(250,000 members)

Army and Air Force Mutual   (800) 336-4538
   Aid Association   (703) 522-3060
468 Sheridan Avenue   (703) 875-0076 Fax
Fort Myer, VA 22211-5002
E-mail: info@aa7maaa.com
(60,000 members)

Association of the U.S. Army   (800) 336-4570
2110 Washington Blvd. #210   (703) 841-4300
Arlington, VA 22204-5711   (703) 243-2589 Fax
E-mail: ausahq@aol.com
(110,000 members)

Blinded Veterans Association   (202) 371-8880
477 H. Street, N.W.   (202) 371-8258 Fax
Washington, DC 20001
(7,400 members)

Catholic War Veterans USA, Inc.   (703) 549-3622
441 N. Lee Street   (703) 684-5196 Fax
Alexandria, VA 22314
(35,000 members)

Congressional Medal of   (803) 884-8862
   Honor Society   (803) 884-1471 Fax
40 Patriots Point Road
Mount Pleasant, SC 29464
(185 members. Send SASE)

Disabled American Veterans   (606) 441-7300
National Headquarters   (606) 441-9521 Fax
PO Box 14301
Cincinnati, OH 45250-0301
(1,000,000 members)

Fleet Reserve Association   (703) 683-1400
125 N. West Street   (703) 549-6610 Fax
Alexandria, VA 22314-2754
(160,000 members)

Gold Star Wives of America   (609) 696-1882
1964 E. Oak Road, Unit I-4   (609) 691-1668 Fax
Vineland, NJ 08360
(13,000 members)

Jewish War Veterans of the USA   (202) 265-6280
1811 "R" Street, N.W.   (202) 234-5662 Fax
Washington, DC 20009
(100,000 members)

The Tailhook Association   (619) 689-9223
9696 Businesspark Avenue   (619) 578-8839 Fax
San Diego, CA 92131-1643
E-mail: thookassn@aol.com
(12,260 members)

Marine Corps Association   (703) 640-6161
PO Box 1775   (703) 640-0823 Fax
Quantico, VA 22134
(110,000 members)

Marine Corps League   (703) 207-9588
8626 Lee Highway, Suite 201   (703) 207-0047 Fax
Fairfax, VA 22031
(44,000 members)

Marine Corps Reserve   (703) 548-7607
  Officers Association
201 N Washington Street, #206
Alexandria, VA 22314
(5,000 members)

Military Chaplains Assn
PO Box 42660
Washington, DC 20015-0660
E-mail: chaplain@charietiesusa.com
(1,550 members)

(717) 642-6792
Phone and Fax

Military Order of the
  Purple Heart of the USA, Inc.
5413-B Backlick Road
Springfield, VA 22151

(703) 642-5360
(703) 642-2054 Fax

Military Order of the World Wars
435 North Lee Street
Alexandria, VA 22314
(14,000 members)

(703) 683-4911
(703) 683-4501 Fax

National Amputation Chapter
73 Church Street
Malverne, NY 11565
(2,500 members)

(516) 887-3600
(516) 887-3667 Fax

National Association for
  Uniformed Services
5535 Hempstead Way
Springfield, VA 22151
E-mail: mconaus@aol.com
(156,000 members)

(703) 750-1342
(703) 354-4380 Fax

National Association of
  Atomic Veterans
PO Box 4424
Salem, MA 01970
(4,000 members)

(800) 784-NAAV
(508) 740-9267 Fax

National Association of
  Fleet Tug Sailors
PO Box 1507
Sausalito, CA 94965-1507
(1,000 members)

(415) 331-7757

National Guard Association   (202) 789-0031
  of the United States
1 Massachusetts Avenue, N.W.
Washington, DC 20001
(51,000 members)

National League of Families of   (202) 223-6846
  American Prisoners and   (202) 785-9410 Fax
  Missing in Southeast Asia
1001 Connecticut Ave, N.W., Ste 219
Washington, DC 20036-5504
E-mail: 76142.611@compuserve.com
(The League can verify whether an individual has been listed
MIA/POW from Vietnam or has returned. Will forward letters
to League family members.)

National Military Family Assn   (703) 823-6632
6000 Stephenson Avenue #304
Alexandria, VA 22304-3526
(6,000 members)

Naval Enlisted Reserve Assn   (703) 534-1329
6703 Farragut Avenue
Falls Church, VA 22042
(16,000 members)

Naval Reserve Association   (703) 548-5800
1619 King Street   (703) 683-3647 Fax
Alexandria, VA 22314
E-mail: deville@navy-reserve.org
(25,000 members)

Navy League of the U.S.   (703) 528-1775
2300 Wilson Blvd
Arlington, VA 22201
(73,000 members)

Navy Mutual Aid Association   (703) 614-1638
Henderson Hall   (703) 695-4635 Fax
29 Carpenter Road
Arlington, VA 22212
(82,000 members)

Non-Commissioned   (210) 653-6161
 Officers Assn
10635H IH35 North
San Antonio, TX 78233
(160,000 members)

Paralyzed Veterans of America   (800) 424-8200
801 18th Street, N.W.   (202) 872-1300
Washington, DC 20006   (202) 785-4452 Fax
(17,216 members)

Pearl Harbor Survivors   (805) 948-1851
 Association, Inc.
Drawer 2598
Lancaster, CA 93539
(10,750 members)

Polish Legion of American   (703) 354-2771
 Veterans of USA
5413-C Backlick Road
Springfield, VA 22151
(16,000 members)

Regular Veterans Assn
 of the U.S., Inc.
5200 Wilkinson Blvd.
Charlotte, NC 28205-5450
(18,000 members)

Reserve Officers Association   (202) 646-7715
 of the United States
One Constitution Ave, N.E.
Washington, DC 20002
(128,000 members)

Retired Enlisted Association   (303) 752-0660
1111 South Abilene Court   (303) 752-0835 Fax
Aurora, CO 80012
E-mail: treah@aol.com
(77,000 members)

The Retired Officers Association   (703) 549-2311
201 N. Washington Street   (703) 838-8173 Fax
Alexandria, VA 22314-2539
E-mail: troa@troa.org
(400,000 members)

Uniformed Service Disabled   (505) 881-4568
  Retirees
5909 Alta Monte, N.E.
Albuquerque, NM 97110
(2,000 members)

U.S. Army Warrant Officers   (703) 742-7727
  Association   (703) 742-7728 Fax
462 Herndon Parkway, #207
Herndon, VA 22070
E-mail: usawoa@erols.com
(5,000 members)

U.S. Coast Guard Cheif Petty   (703) 941-0395
  Officers National Office
5520–G Hempstead Way
Springfield, VA 22151

U.S. Naval Home   (800) 332-3527
1800 Beach Drive
Gulfport, MS 38507-1587
(500 residents)

U.S. Soldiers & Airmen's Home   (800) 422-9988
3700 N. Capitol Street, N.W.
Washington, DC 20317-0001
(1,600 residents)

U.S. Submarine Veterans   (630) 834-2718
  of WWII
862 Chatham Avenue
Elmhurst, IL 60126-4531

Veterans of the   (703) 528-4058
  Battle of the Bulge
PO Box 11129
Arlington, VA 22210-2129
(11,000 members)

Veterans of Foreign Wars   (816) 756-3390
  of the U.S.   (816) 968-1169 Fax
406 W. 34th Street, Suite 523
Kansas City, MO 64111
(2,000,000 members. Two names per request.)

Veterans of the Vietnam War, Inc.   (717) 825-7215
760 Jumper Road   (717) 825-8223 Fax
Wilkes-Barre, PA 18702-8033
(30,000 members)

Veterans of World War One   (703) 780-5660
  of the USA, Inc.   (703) 780-8465 Fax
PO Box 8027
Alexandria, VA 22306-8027
(6,000 members)

Vietnam Helicopter Pilots Assn   (800) 505-VHPA
949 University Avenue, Suite 210   (916) 648-1072 Fax
Sacramento, CA 95825
(8,000 members. Will not forward letters; advertise "searches.")

Vietnam Veterans of   (202) 628-2700
  America, Inc.   (202) 628-5880 Fax
1224 M Street, N.W.
Washington, DC 20005
(45,000 members)

Vietnam Veterans Wives   (509) 775-2220
PO Box 396
Republic, WA 99166

Directory of Military Reunion Associations

Air Force and Army Air Force Associations

8th Air Force
  Historical Society
PO Box 7215
St Paul, MN 55107-7215
(800) 833-1942

11th Air Force Assn
1290 Cody Street
Lakewood, CO80215-4897
(303) 237-0620

13th Air Force Assn
7049 W. Illinois Road
Ludington, MI 49431-9503
(616) 843-9597

14th Air Force Assn
32267 Phantom Drive
Rancho Palos, CA 90274
(310) 377-5814

Air Weather Assn
1879 Cole Road
Aromas, CA 95004-9617
(408) 726-1660

Bombardiers, Inc.
500 Jackson Street, #1407
Daphne, AL 36526
(334) 626-3920

CBI Hump Pilots Assn
808 Lester Street
Poplar Bluff, MO 63901-4934
(314) 785-2420

Order of Daedalians, Inc.
PO Box 249
Randolph AFB, TX 78148
(210) 945-2111

Army Associations

1st Armored Division Assn
PO Box 211609
Augusta, GA 30917-1609
(706) 860-6467

1st Cavalry Division Assn
302 North Main Street
Copperas Cove, TX 76522
(800) 234-9313

1st Infantry Division Assn
Bldg 405
Ft Riley, KS 66442
(913) 239-3032

2nd Armored Division Assn
8053 Highpoint Blvd.
Brooksville, FL 34613-7346
(904) 596-6843

2nd Infantry Division Assn
PO Box 460
Buda, TX 78610-0460
(512) 295-5324

3rd Armored Division Assn
PO Box 61743
Phoenix, AZ 85082-1473
(602) 840-0398

4th Armored Division Assn
1823 Shady Drive
Farrell, PA 16121-1342
(412) 342-6058

5th Armored Division Assn
13344 Luthman Road
Minster, OH 45865-9327
(419) 628-4032

6th Armored Division Assn
PO Box 5011
Louisville, KY 40255-5011
(502) 451-9822

6th Infantry Division Assn
622 W. Birch Avenue
Fergus Falls, MN 56537-1318
(218) 739-2797

7th Armored Division Assn
23218 Springbrook Drive
Farmington Hills, MI 48336-3371
(810) 476-0777

7th Infantry Division Assn
7303 "H" Street
Little Rock, AR 72205-2636
(501) 663-4622

8th Armored Division Assn
12834 Paintbrush Drive
Sun City West, AZ 86375-2551
(602) 584-5967

9th Infantry Division Assn
412 Gregory Avenue
Weekawken, NJ 07087-5602
(201) 866-8195

10th Armored Division Assn
9807 Main Street
Bay Port, MI 48720-9782
(517) 656-3551

11th ABN/Air Assault
125 Lexington Drive
Clarksville, TN 37042-3651
(615) 552-7761

11th ACR Vets of
   Vietnam & Cambodia
927 Mulberry Lane
Kohler, WI 53044-1469
(414) 457-4611

11th Armored Div. Assn
2328 Admiral Street
Aliquippa, PA 15001-2204
(412) 375-6295

12th Armored Division
242 Olympic Court
Leicester, NC 28748-6328
(704) 683-9466

13th Armored Div. Assn
204 Edgewood Place
Ferndale, MI 48220-2467
(810) 547-6562

14th Armored Division
42 Vestal Avenue
Binghamton, NY 13903-1318
(607) 724-1958

16th Armored Div. Assn
PO Box 222
Lake Alfred, FL 33850
(813) 956-3327

23rd Infantry Division Assn
427 Willow Street
W. Roxbury, MA 02132-1326
(617) 323-2007

24th Infantry Div. Assn
14030 Xanthus Lane
Rogers, MN 55374-3992
(612) 427-2433

25th Infantry Division Assn
PO Box 746
Rocklin, CA 95677-0746
(916) 624-3244

29th Infantry Div. Assn
130 Union Road
Coatesville, PA 19320-1329
(610) 384-2404

30th Infantry Division Assn
83 Brussels Court
Toms River, NJ 08757-5822
(908) 505-6079

33rd Infantry Div. Assn
PO Box 350
Hansville, WA 98340
(206) 638-1926

35th Infantry Division Assn
4311 Womack Drive
Colorado Springs, CO 80915
(719) 596-3369

36th Infantry Div. Assn
PO Box 2049
Malakoff, TX 75148-2049
(903) 489-1644

38th Infantry Division Assn
1791 Lockerbie Drive
Columbus, IN 47203-4038
(812) 372-1382

40th Infantry Division Assn
210 Highland Avenue
Maybrook, NY 12543-1012
(914) 427-2320

41st Infantry Division Assn
PO Box 2277
Beaverton, OR 97075-2277
(503) 646-7890.

44th Infantry Division Assn
614 S. Crea
Decatur, IL 62522-3248
(217) 428-0069

45th Infantry Division Assn
2145 N.E. 36th Street
Oklahoma City, OK 73111-5302
(210) 681-9134

63rd Infantry Division Assn
5745 Viau Way
Zephyr Hills, FL 33540-8544
(813) 788-2499

65th Infantry Division Assn
7300 Marshall Road
Upper Darby, PA 19082-4820
(610) 622-3139

69th Infantry Division Assn
218 Sacred Heart Lane
Reisterstown, MD 21126-1414
(410) 833-2771

70th Infantry Division Assn
5825 Horton
Mission, KS 66202-2608
(913) 722-2024

71st Infantry Division Assn
14801 Grapeland Avenue
Cleveland, OH 44111-2132
(216) 251-8257

75th Infantry Division Assn
4105 75th Street
Des Moines, IA 50322-2251
(515) 278-0081

78th Infantry Division Assn
1122 Edward Terrace
St. Louis, MO 63117-1521
(314) 847-3930

82nd ABN Division Assn
5459 Northcutt Place
Dayton, OH 45414-3742
(513) 898-5977

83rd Infantry Division Assn
3749 Stahlheber Road
Hamilton, OH 45013-8907
(513) 863-2199

86th Infantry Division Assn
1226 Kilian Blvd. S.E.
Saint Cloud, MN 56304-1645
(612) 252-9579

87th Infantry Division Assn
2374 N. Dundee Court
Highland, MI 48357-3716
(313) 887-9005

88th Infantry Division Assn
PO Box 6510
Albany, CA 94706-0510
(510) 526-0385

90th Infantry Division Assn
PO Box 730
South Hill, VA 23970-0730
(800) 416-9090

91st Infantry Division Assn
5220 Vincent Avenue, South
Minneapolis, MN 55410-2420
(612) 926-4305

94th Infantry Division Assn
609 Dogwood Drive
Downingtown, PA 19335
(215) 363-7826

95th Infantry Division Assn
8032 S. 86th Court
Justice, IL 60458-1445
(708) 458-3047

96th Infantry Division Assn
7634 Fielding
Detroit, MI 48228-3232
(313) 271-5778

100th Infantry Division
1503 Creswood Road
Philadelphia, PA 19115-3110
(215) 698-1772

101st Airbn Division Assn
PO Box 101
Bentonville, OH 45105-0101
(513) 549-4326

102nd Infantry Div. Assn
1406 Abbot Street
Muncie, IN 47303-2757
(317) 289-1714

103rd Infantry Division Assn
8260 Moreland Road
Jerome, MI 49249-9705
(517) 688-9249

104th Infantry Div. Assn
10406 Harriett Avenue, S.
Bloomington, MN 55420
(612) 888-1250

106th Infantry Division Assn
1103 Arbor Glen Circle
Winter Springs, FL 32708
(407) 695-6164

187th Airborne RCT
RR 1, Box 311 A
Cumberland, VA 23040
(804) 492-5827

511th Para Infantry Assn
618 Far Hills Drive
E. Peoria, IL 61611-1009
(309) 699-0077

511th Pir Assn
32 W. 34th Street
Bayonne, NJ 07002-391149
(201) 436-3488

Army Aviation Assn of
  America, (Quad A)
Richmondville Avenue
Westport, CT 06880
(203) 226-8184

Vietnam Helicopter Crew-
  members Association
PO Box 2592
Memphis, TN 38175
(901) 795-2850

Marine Corps Associations

1st Marine Division Assn
14325 Willard Road, #107
Chantilly, VA 22021
(703) 803-3195

2nd Marine Division Assn
35 Ashwell Avenue
Rocky Hill, CT 06067-2415
(203) 563-6149

3rd Marine Division Assn
978 Larkspur Place N
Mt Laurel, NJ 08054-4952
(609) 235-8178

4th Marine Division Assn
PO Box 595
Laurel, FL 34272-0595

5th Marine Division Assn
362 Roosevelt Avenue
Salt Lake City, UT 84115-5120
(801) 466-8991

6th Marine Division Assn
234 Belden Drive
Edwardsville, IL 62025-3179
(618) 692-4655

China Marine Assn
14 Magnolia Lane
Wildwood, FL 34785-9385
(904) 748-3671

The Marine Raider Assn
4119 43rd Avenue, W
Bradenton, FL 34205-2343
(813) 756-2564

MC Air Traffic Control Assn
1936 River Bend Rd
Heber Springs, AR 72543-8562
(501) 362-3008

MC Air Transport Assn
PO Box 59765
Dallas, TX 75243-1765
(214) 235-6607

MC Amtrac Assn
3 Potomac St
Boonsboro, MD 21713-1223
(301) 432-5289

MC Avaiation Assn
PO Box 296
Quantico MCB, VA 22134
(800) 336-0291

MC Aviation Recon Assn
PO Box 22581
St Petersburg, FL 33742-2581

MC Combat Correspondents
19701 Gulf Boulevard
Indian Shores Bch, FL 34635
(813) 595-5977

MC Counter Intel Assn
PO Box 3029
Virginia Beach, VA 23454-3029
(804) 481-6163

MC Drill Instructors Assn
1307 21st Street
Port Huron, MI 48060-5513
(810) 982-2530

MC Intelligence Assn
PO Box 4602
Oceanside, CA 92052-4602
(619) 392-0924

MC Mustang Assn
PO Box 1314
Delran, NJ 08075
(800) 321-8762

MC Tankers Assn
12 Makah Way
La Conner, WA 98257-9504
(360) 466-3080

Navy and Coast Guard Associations

CG Combat Vets Assn
PO Box 544
Westfield Ctr, OH 44251-0544
(216) 725-6527

Corpsmen United
PO Box 722
Anacortes, WA 98221-0722
(360) 293-5873

Destroyer Escort Sailors Assn
PO Box 680085
Orlando, FL 32868-0085
(407) 877-7671

Destroyer Mine Force
338 S. La Serena Drive
W. Covina, CA 91791-2215
(818) 339-7965

LSM-LSMR Assn
66 Summer Street
Greenfield, MA 01301-1463
(413) 774-2397

National CPO Assn
106 Waring–Welfare Road
Boerne, TX 78006-7925
(210) 537-4899

National LSM Association
PO Box 575
Raynham, MA 02768

Naval Mine Warfare Assn
224 Angelus Drive
Salinas, CA 93906-3302
(408) 449-5325

Navy Nurse Corps Assn
1225 19th St., N.W., 5th Floor
Washington, DC 20036-2410
(202) 828-7040

Navy Scouting Sqdns Assn
7433 Oakleaf Drive
Santa Rosa, CA 95409-6207
(707) 438-0236

Navy Seabees Veterans
3124 Arborside Drive
Las Vegas, NV 89117-2271
(702) 254-7000

Patrol Craft Sailors Assn
132 Lakeside Circle, North
Fort Myers, FL 33903-5642
(813) 997-3318

Patrol Frigate Sailors Assn
5272 Dorris Drive
Arnold, MO 63010

PT Boats, Inc.
PO Box 38070
Germantown, TN 38183
(901) 775-8410

Sharkhunters International
PO Box 1539
Hernando, FL 34442-1539
(904) 637-2917

Tin Can Sailors, Inc.
PO Box 100
Somerset, MA 02726

Transport Sailors Assn
PO Box 732
New Paltz, NY 12561-0732
(914) 255-5703

U.S. LST Association
PO Box 167438
Oregon, OH 43616
(800) 228-5870

U.S. Navy Memorial Foundat'n
PO Box 48817
Arlington, VA 22209-8728

USS Alabama
PO Box 501
Keller, TX 76244-0501
(817) 431-2424

USS Arkansas
PO Box 974
Geyserville, CA 95441
(707) 857-4029

USS California/Marine Det
616 W. Lafayette
Staunton, IL 62088-1042
(618) 635-5638

USS Colorado
PO Box 153
Ridgefield, WA 98642-0153
(360) 887-8669

USS Idaho Assn
PO Box 711247
San Diego, CA 92171-1247
(619) 271-6106

USS Iowa Veterans Assn
619 Stafford Avenue
Spartanburg, SC 29302-4509
(803) 582-4640

USS LCI Reunions
643 Callery Road
Evans City, PA 16033-3007
(412) 538-8151

USS Maryland
1478 La Corta Cir
Lemon Grove, CA 91945-4317
(619) 469-3142

USS Massachusetts Assn
PO Box 455
Waltham, MA 02254-0455
(617) 899-9198

USS Mississippi
6099 Overseas Hwy W 81
Marathon, FL 33050-2750
(305) 289-7540

USS Missouri
18 Ingleside Avenue
Norwalk, CT 06850-2522
(203) 846-9758

USS Nevada
27224 Cornell Street
Hemet, CA 92344-8264
(909) 925-1714

USS Nevada
2125 Swannanoa Avenue
Kingsport, TN 37664-3222
(615) 246-2225

USS New Jersey Vets Inc.
281 Autumn Trace
Port Orange, FL 32119-7802
(904) 788-1459

USS New Mexico
10513 Repose Drive
St. Louis, MO 63137-2232
(314) 867-2747

USS New York
1 Lake Lorraine Dr
Belleville, IL 62221-2475
(618) 235-4678

USS Oklahoma Assn
PO Box 104
Cushman, AR 72526-0104
(501) 793-7084

USS Pennsylvania
8040 Butterweed Drive
Colorado Springs, CO 80920
(719) 599-9281

USS Tennessee & Marine Det
PO Box 1174
Willow Grove, PA 19090-0704
(215) 784-9885

USS Utah Assn
5000 Adair Way
San Jose, CA 95124-5341
(408) 356-4092

USS West Virginia
PO Box 442
Big Bear City, CA 92314-0442
(909) 585-3448

USS North Carolina
1638 S.E. 39th Terrace
Cape Coral, FL 33904-5024
(941) 945-6597

USS Pennsylvania
3053 Birchfield Drive
Memphis, TN 38127-7403
(901) 357-0263

USS South Dakota Assn
1210 N. 12th Street
Norfolk, NE 68701-2729
(402) 371-0242

USS Texas
RR 4, Box 2122
Plymouth, NH 03264-9448
(603) 536-2403

USS Washington
PO Box 13047
Columbus, OH 43213-0047

USS Wisconsin
PO Box 64
Rudolph, Wi 54475-0064
(715) 435-3282

All Services Associations

Assn of Ex-POW of the
  Korean War
PO Box 120993
Arlington, TX 76012
(817) 460-4919

Chosin Few International
10105 SE 96th Avenue
Portland, OR 97266-7202
(503) 777-2947

CBI Veterans Assn
145 Pendleton Drive
Athens, GA 30606-1644
(404) 542-3189

Counterparts Advisors/VN
100 Red Oak Circle
Temple, TX 76502
(817) 773-6520

Iwo Jima Veterans Reunion
594 Old Hwy 27
Vicksburg, MS 39180-8820
(601) 636-1861

Korean War Veterans Assn
117 Mark Drive
Fairview Heights, IL 62208
(800) 603-6555

USS LST Assn
PO Box 167438
Oregon, OH 43616-7438
(800) 228-5870

The addresses of many reunion associations change periodically with the election of new officers or reunion organizers. To obtain the current address of any of the above reunion organizations or of the over 6,000 other reunion organizations, contact:

National Reunion Registry and Press Service
PO Box 355
Bulverde, TX 78163-0355
(210) 438-4177, (210) 438-4114 Fax

Sample Letter
(See page 94 for text reference)

(Date)

Veteran Organization
111 Some Street
Sometown, USA 55555

Ladies/Gentlemen:

The Purpose of this letter is to ask your assistance in locating my brother, John Paul Smith. I have not seen nor heard from him in five years. It is extremely important that I contact him.

John was born on January 1, 1939. He served in the Navy from 1959 to 1964 as a Chief Petty Officer. He was a member of the Naval Reserve from 1964 to 1968. In 1968 he was appointed a Warrant officer in the Transportation Corps of the Army. He was discharged in 1971.

I would appreciate it if you would check your files and determine if he was or is a member of your organization. If so, please advise me of his current address. If your policy prohibits giving out his address, please forward this letter to him.

If you do not have any records on him, please include a notice in your magazine or newsletter stating that I am trying to locate him or anyone who knows his location.

I learned about this service your organization provides from the book "How to Locate Anyone Who Is or Has Been in the Military." Thank you for your assistance.

Sincerely,

(Name)

Chapter 6

LOCATING WOMEN VETERANS

This chapter describes the methods available to locate women veterans and includes background information on women in the military. There are several ways to locate women veterans who have married and changed their last name. Some of the methods include:

- *The Department of Veterans Affairs*
- *National Personnel Records Center*
- *Armed Forces World-Wide Locators*
- *Major veterans organizations*
- *Women's veterans organizations*
- *Computer searches*

Brief History of Women in the Military

In 1901 the U.S. Army established the Nursing Corps as an auxiliary unit for women. The Navy followed in 1908. These women wore uniforms and were official members of the U.S. Military.

Women in World War I

Approximately thirteen thousand women served in the Naval Reserve and Marine Corps Reserve during World War I and were given the rank of Yeomen (F). This term described those who held clerical jobs and F meant *female.* Women in WWI served stateside as well as overseas duty. There were two hundred women killed during this war.

After the war ended, most women returned to civilian life but were granted the same veteran benefits as men.

Women in World War II

In 1942 the armed forces established auxiliary corps for women for all branches of the armed forces. In 1948 the *Women's Armed Services Integration Act* allowed women to serve with the same military status as men. However, certain restrictions applied such as no women in combat. Over 400,000 women served during WWII.

Army: In 1942 the U.S. Army began the *Women's Army Auxiliary Corps* (WAAC) and was renamed *Women's Army Corps* (WAC) in 1943. About 100,000 women served in the WAC.

Coast Guard: *Semper Paratis, Always Ready* (SPAR) was the auxiliary service established for women in the Coast Guard in Word War II.

Marine Corps: They created the *Women's Reserve* during World War I. They are simply referred to as Women Marines.

Navy: The Naval counterpart was *Women Accept-ed for Volunteer Emergency Service* (WAVES). The acronym is retained as an unofficial nickname.

Women Civilians in WWII

Women Air Service Pilots (WASP) was a group of U.S. civilian pilots under contract in World War II. Over 1,000 women pilots served as test pilots, in-structors, ran target missions and ferried new aircraft to military bases overseas. Thirty-eight of these women died during WWII. The WASP was disband-ed in 1944. In 1977, they received military status and eligibility for veteran's benefits.

Locating Women Veterans

Women veterans are usually more difficult to lo-cate than their male counterparts. This is because many former women members of the armed forces marry and assume a new surname. If you know the individual's married name, then you can locate the person in the same manner as male veterans. If you do not know the person's new surname, the search can be difficult. In addition to the individual's name, the following identifying information makes a search much easier. These are service number, Social Secu-rity number, date or year of birth, former unit or base assigned and former addresses. Methods to ob-tain and find people with this information is dis-cussed throughout this book. It will be helpful for you to read the rest of this book.

The Department of Veterans Affairs (VA)

The VA will probably have the woman's married name if she is receiving VA benefits. They will be able to identify her with a maiden name and some of the following: SSN; service number; VA claim number or date of birth. If they can identify her, they will provide her new surname. They will also tell you the location of her VA file. She will usually live within three hundred miles of the VA Regional Office that has her file. With this information, do a search of the National Telephone Directory or call the telephone information operator in the general area of the VA Regional Office.

If you know her service number or date of birth, you might obtain her SSN from the VA Records Processing Center. See Chapter Five for details. You can also have a letter forwarded to her through the VA. In some cases you can obtain her date of birth from the VA, if you know her service number or SSN. The VA can also tell you if the individual is deceased.

National Personnel Records Center (NPRC)

The NPRC enters names of veterans into their index with the name used when the veteran was discharged (after separation from either active duty or the reserves). The NPRC will forward a letter to her under certain circumstances (see Chapter Five for details). The address of the veteran is usually the one used when the veteran separated from the service or reserve. If the veteran was contacted by the NPRC for any reason, then the most current address will be used.

You may also request her military records under the Freedom of Information Act if her service number or SSN is known. These records usually contain her date of birth. A date of birth can be used for a driver license search or a date of birth search. (See computer searches below and Appendix B).

Armed Forces World-Wide Locator

Women who are currently on active duty, members of the reserves and National Guard and those who are retired may be located or contacted through the appropriate branch locator. (See Chapters Two, Three and Four for information.)

Major Veterans Organization

Hundreds of thousands of women veterans are members of major veterans organizations, such as the VFW, DAV, The American Legion, etc. These women can often be located through these organizations. (See Chapter Five for a list of major veterans organizations.)

Women's Veterans Organizations

The following women's veterans organizations can assist in locating women who served in the military. Most of these associations/organizations list women by both their maiden name and married name. They will either provide an address or forward a letter. There is usually no fee for this service.

Retired Army Nurse Corps Assn   (210) 824-0329
PO Box 39235
San Antonio, TX 78218

Society of Retired Air Force Nurses   (210) 494-1096
PO Box 681026
San Antonio, TX 78268

WAVES National   (706) 663-8253
444 Moore Rd
Pine Mountain, GA 31822

Women Air Force Service Pilots   (210) 822-7937
2215 Camelback Drive
San Antonio, TX 78209-4261

Women's Army Corps   (205) 820-4019
  Veterans Association
PO Box 5577
Fort McClellan, AL 36205

Women's Marine Association
PO Box 387
Quantico, VA 22134-0387

Women's Overseas Service League   (210) 656-1697
414 Windcrest
San Antonio, TX 78239

Women in the Air Force   (313) 331-7966
9000 E. Jefferson Avenue
Detroit, MI 48214-2959

Military Women Officers   (813) 634-2894
1010 American Eagle
Sun City Center, FL 33573-5273

N.E. Conference of Navy Women   (207) 439-6573
89 Mobile Manor
Kittery, ME 03904-5591

Waves/Spars/Nurses   (216) 331-8074
3465 Chrisfield Dr
Cleveland, OH 44116-3731

Women Who Served   (916) 393-2349
  in the Military
1625-B Meadowview Road
Sacramento, CA 95832-1037

WWII Flight Nurses Association   (352) 787-6064
02111 Spring Lake Road
Fruitland Park, FL 34731-5254

Air Force Women   (210)493-8689
  Officers Association
4323 Shavano Woods
San Antonio, TX 78249-1845

Navy Nurse Corps Association   (210) 828-7040
1225 19th Street, S.W. 5th Floor
Washington, DC 20036-2410

Black Women In Service   (210) 656-4961
5002 Village Lawn
San Antonio, TX 78218-3837

All Navy Women's   (407) 345-0435
  National Alliance
PO Box 147
Goldenrod, FL 32733-0147

Women in Military Service for America

The Women in Military Service Memorial Foundation seeks women veterans to include in its computer database. Authorized by Congress in 1986, the Memorial, to be built with private donations, will be located at the main entrance of Arlington National

Cemetery. It will include a computer registry with the names and service histories of as many of the nation's 1.8 million women veterans as possible. The database will also include photographs of women in uniform and their own narratives of their most memorable experiences. They will be registered by both maiden and married name and by hometown. You can assist the Memorial by identifying women veterans for inclusion in the Registry. When completed, the Memorial will become another resource for locating women veterans. The foundation has registered approximately 150,000 military women to date. The organization does not release the addresses of individuals registered with the Memorial, but can, on a limited basis, forward correspondence. There is no cost for this service, but donations are accepted. For information on registration and how to donate:

> Women in Military Service for
>   America Memorial Foundation, Inc.
> 5510 Columbia Pike Street #302
> Arlington, VA 22204
> (800) 222-2294, (703) 533-1155
> (703) 931-4208 Fax

Vietnam Women's Memorial Project, Inc.

On November 11, 1993, the Vietnam Women's Memorial Project dedicated the first memorial in the nation's capital honoring military and civilian women who served our country. The bronze statue portrays three women and a wounded male soldier and stands near the wall of names at the Vietnam Veterans Memorial in Washington, DC. Its quiet grace, strength and dignity reflect that of the thousands of women who served during the Vietnam war.

The VWMP welcomes home Vietnam women veterans. The project thanks women who throughout the ages have tended to the wounded and provided support wherever and whenever they could. The project puts women veterans in touch with ongoing research on the after-effects of war—sociological, psychological, and epidemiological.

The VWMP has a database of 12,000 women veterans and civilians who served in Vietnam. They will forward letters on a limited basis. Contact them to register or to make a donation.

Vietnam Women's Memorial Project, Inc.
2001 "S" Street, N.W., Suite 302
Washington, DC 20009
(202) 328-7253, (202) 986-3636 Fax

Computer Searches

There are several computer searches that can help locate a woman if a married surname is not available. These computer searches are:

Social Security number search: If you know the individual's SSN, this search will provide her current surname and most current reported address.

Date of Birth search: If you provide the individual's first name and DOB, the computer will list everyone in the database with a matching first name and DOB. The report includes first name and last name, city and state of residence, and DOB. This search can sometimes provide a street address, telephone number and SSN. *There are usually only a few* *matches with this search.* It is the most effective computer search to determine someone's current surname and address. This search can save a searcher numerous hours of research time and money.

The Social Security Master Death Index: If you provide the individual's first name and DOB, the computer will provide first and last names of all matching individuals along with their date of death and place of death.

All of these computer searches are described in detail in Appendix B.

Chapter 7

LOCATING VETERANS FOR A REUNION

Other parts of this book give all the necessary steps to find veterans for a reunion. This chapter summarizes these steps for you and also adds a few special tips for reunion planners.

Steps for Reunion Planners

The Armed Forces switched from using Service Numbers to using Social Security numbers as a means of identification on the following dates:

Army and Air Force	July 1969
Navy and Marine Corps	July 1972
Coast Guard	Oct. 1974

We mention this because finding veterans with Social Security numbers is much easier than finding those with service numbers. This is because Social Security numbers are in almost all databases, not just military-related databases. In fact it is wise to collect (or verify) SSNs from all those in your group who are "found." That way it is easier to find them again if they get "lost."

The main difference in search techniques is that a SSN trace can be done sooner and more effectively on those veterans who can be identified by their SSN. Ninety percent of the time a Social Security trace will provide the most current reported address from the header information of 160 million credit files. If the individual is deceased, the date of death will usually be reported. Request a brochure and a group price list from the Nationwide Locator (see Appendix B). Then:

- Obtain a unit roster or ship muster roll from the National Archives or appropriate military service (see Chapter Eight). These contain the name, rank and service number of all members (if they were prepared before the services converted from service numbers to Social Security numbers). The Army rosters from 1944, 1945 and 1946 were destroyed. For these years, create a roster from morning reports, unit and individual orders, and payrolls. By using all of these, you will accumulate a "master" list with correct spelling and legal names, service numbers and ranks of all of the people you want to contact.

- For those who served after the "switch" dates, these unit rosters or ship musters contain the name, rank and SSN of enlisted and sometimes officers assigned to that unit or ship on the date the document was prepared. The SSNs will be marked out. Sometimes the marking can be removed to reveal the SSN.

The 11th Armored Cavalry's Veterans of Vietnam and Cambodia collected unit orders which contained names and SSNs. With the help of the Nationwide Locator (Appendix B) they located over 16,000 of their former members in three years. This is the fastest growing reunion association in the country. With the increase of revenue from dues from new members, they have paid for all locating costs and have increased the amount in their treasury substantially.

- If you cannot locate an address for a veteran through a Social Security trace, you may need to search the Social Security Death Index to see if the veteran has died. Copies of the SSA Master Death Index on CD ROM are located in some main libraries and many family history libraries.
- If you cannot find a service number or a Social Security number for a veteran, search one of the National Telephone Directories.
- Register your reunion with VETS (see page 141) and the National Reunion Registry (see page 142).
- Prepare a good news release or reunion notice. Make it as brief as possible, but be sure to include your organization, branch of service, the war or period of time, name, address and telephone number of the reunion organizer, date and place of the reunion. See page 143.
- Send reunion notices or news releases to all appropriate veterans organizations and request that they be published in their magazines, bulletins and newsletters. Use the CO-OP mail program provided by the National Reunion Registry and Press Service which sends notice of your reunion

to over 2,400 newspapers, public libraries and veterans organizations (see page 142).

- Prepare a letter or news release informing each individual about your organization or the scheduled reunion. Have the Veterans Administration Records Processing Center forward these letters to former unit members. See page 88.

- Check with each individual that you have located to see if he knows addresses or locations of other missing members.

- Have individuals you have found search their own files, footlockers, scrapbooks, letters, etc, for any orders. Orders (unit orders, reassignment orders, orders for promotions, awards, etc.) are very valuable because they contain the correct spelling of the names, service numbers and SSNs. Ask for copies of all these orders.

- Check appropriate Officers Registers for information on unit or ship officers—such as date of birth, service number, SSN, state where they entered service. See Chapters Five and Eight.

- Have the retired locator of the appropriate service branch forward letters to individuals who have retired from the service. See Chapter Four.

- If you know the city and state where the veteran entered the service, contact the postmaster, mayor, historical organizations, veterans organizations, churches, schools and reunion groups of that city or town and ask if they have the current location of the veteran or his family.

- Attempt to locate individuals who may belong to veterans organizations, e.g., VFW, DAV, The American Legion, AMVETS, The Retired Officers Association, NCO Association, Fleet Reserve Association, Marine Corps League, etc. See Chapter Five.

- http://www.switchboard.com is a National Telephone Directory web site run by a mailing list company. It lists the names, addresses and telephone numbers of 100 million people.
- Contact all the appropriate high school, college and university alumni associations for the addresses of veterans who may have attended their schools. If the alumni association will not supply you with an address, contact the college library and ask if they have directories of former students. Ask the librarian to give you the individual's address.
- Continue to advertise your reunion. Have individuals send news releases to their local newspapers. Put notices of your reunion on computer bulletin board services. Use specialty advertising such as bumper stickers, T-shirts, baseball caps, badges, etc, which show your reunion organization, telephone number and date of reunion.
- Establish a page on the World Wide Web advertising your reunion. Link this page with veterans group pages.

Reunions for Desert Storm, Grenada, Panama and Bosnia

If you were involved in any of these military activities or have friends or relatives who were, preparation for a future military reunion should be done now. The following steps are recommended:

- Appoint one or more people who were in the units involved to be reunion organizers.
- Collect rosters of the unit that include names, ranks, dates of birth, and Social Security numbers of the members.
- Obtain home addresses of all members through the Nationwide Locator (see Appendix B).
- Place all information in a computer database.
- Keep in touch with all original unit members by letter or a newsletter at least once a year.
- Prepare for your reunion now. Select a site and date and inform all members.
- Seek donations from unit members to defray mailing and organizational costs.
- Register your reunion organization as soon as possible with:
  a. National Reunion Registry (see page 142)
  b. The American Legion's VETS (see page 141)
- Subscribe to *Reunions magazine.*

If the above recommendations are completed now, it will be easier to locate all former unit members, and future reunions will be easier to conduct and will have greater participation.

Reunions magazine

Reunions magazine is the only national publication whose focus is reunions of all kinds. In addition to articles on searching, genealogical research and military reunions, there are also tips, leads and suggestions to help in searching for missing people, adoptees and birthparents. The magazine is published quarterly ($24 per year) and includes a workbook. Sample copies available for $2 shipping.

Reunions magazine
PO Box 11727
Milwaukee, WI 53211-0727
(414) 263-4567, (414) 263-6331 Fax
E-mail: reunions@execpc.com
http://www.execpc.com/~reunions

Seeker Magazine

"The Seeker" is an online magazine specializing in reunions, reuniting adoptees with birth parents, locating beneficiaries of wills and insurance policies, etc. There is an ad section where you can post a "looking for" ad at no cost. Areas include "military seeking," "seeking military brats," "generally seeking," and "seeking classmates."

Seeker Magazine
http://www.the-seeker.com

Veterans Electronic Telecommunication Service

The *American Legion Magazine* subscribes to VETS, a telephone and computer service that provides information about military reunions. Dial (900) 737-VETS for dates of reunions and how to contact the reunion organizers. The call costs $1.95 per minute. Hours are 12 noon to 8 p.m. VETS has listings on 15,000 reunion organizations. For free registration write:

VETS
PO Box 1055
Indianapolis, IN 46206
(900) 737-VETS

The National Reunion Registry and Press Service

The National Reunion Registry is a database of over 6,000 military reunion organizations and their reunion planners. Reunion organizers may list their reunions free of charge. Persons seeking reunions can request a records search at no charge. Send a self-addressed stamped envelope along with information about the reunion being sought.

Military reunion organizers may want to use the National Reunion Press Service and the CO-OP mail program to publicize their reunion. For a one-time charge of $60 (less than 3 cents per release) a notice of your reunion is sent to over 2,400 demographically selected outlets. These include veterans associations, civilian and military newspapers, VA facilities, Veterans Service Officers, and public libraries. User testimonials report this is both a successful and cost-effective way to reach long-lost shipmates and buddies.

National Reunion Registry
  and Press Service
PO Box 355
Bulverde, TX 78163-0355
(210) 438-4177, (210) 438-4114 Fax

Sample News Release
(See page 137 for text reference)

101st Mess Kit Repair Battalion
555 Nowhere Street
Sometown, USA 22222-2222
U.S. Army — WWII

For Immediate Release
Contact: John Doe, (555) 555-5555

The United States Army (WWII) 101st
Mess Kit Repair Battalion will hold
its first reunion on September 5,
19____, at the Waldorf Astoria Hotel
in New York City. Former members,
widows, children, or relatives are
asked to contact John Doe, Reunion
Organizer at 123 Maple Street, Any-
town, USA 11111 (555) 555-5555.

-End-

Chapter 8

OBTAINING MILITARY RECORDS

This chapter describes how you can obtain:
- *Individual military records*
- *Unit and Ship records*
- *Unit and Ship histories*
- *Organization records*

Records of Current, Retired and Former Members of the Military

Current and former members of the military (or next of kin, if deceased) can obtain copies of their complete military personnel and medical records. (Next of kin may be grandson, great-grand daughter, etc., in the case of military members who have been dead for several years.) A request should be made on a Standard Form 180 (see Appendix A) or by type-written letter if the form is not available. There is usually no fee for this type of request. It should be sent to the appropriate address listed at the end of this section. No reason is required for requesting the records, but all requests citing medical emergencies and VA claims are processed first.

To ensure that all documents in the file are provided, the request should state, in Section II, Item 1, the exact items being requested. For example: "provide all information in my military personnel file to include unit orders, awards and commendations, any derogatory information, efficiency reports and ratings, promotion orders, assignment and reassignment orders, photographs and qualification records." Be sure to list any other documents the individual remembers being in his records. Only those items specifically named will be provided.

To obtain a complete copy of health records, the veteran should state that he needs them for review by his physician. If he needs information relating to a specific illness or injury suffered while in the military, he should ask for those documents pertaining to that illness or injury. Also, if inpatient (hospitalization) records are needed, he should furnish the approximate dates of hospitalization and the name or number of the hospital, as these records are filed separately from the individual's military records at the National Personnel Records Center.

Due to the Freedom of Information Act, anyone (civilian or military) may receive limited information from the military personnel records of current, former or deceased members of the military. The following information (if available) can be provided.

- Rank/grade
- Name
- Duty status
- Date of rank

- Service number
- Date of birth
- Dependents (including name, sex and age)
- Gross salary
- Geographical location of duty assignments
- Future assignments (approved)
- Unit or office telephone number
- Source of commission (officers)
- Military and civilian education level
- Promotion sequence number
- Awards and decorations
- Official photograph
- Record of court-martial trials (unless classified)
- City/town/state of last known residence; date of that address
- Places of induction and separation

Place of birth, date and location of death, and place of burial of deceased veterans can also be released.

Because of recent changes to the Freedom of Information Act regulations, the armed forces may not provide date of birth, official photo, records of court-martial of members on active duty or in the reserve or National Guard. The NPRC will provide those items.

Because of the Privacy Act, the general public will not be provided with medical information, Social Security number or present address of any current or former living member of the military.

Records are received at the National Personnel Records Center normally 6–24 months after the individual is discharged, completes reserve obligation or retires.

All requests for information made under the Freedom of Information Act should include "ATTN: FOIA Office" in the address, letter, and on the SF 180, if pertaining to current active duty, reserve, National Guard or retired personnel.

A Standard Form 180 (SF 180) is included in Appendix A. This form or a photocopy may be used. If possible, enlarge the form to 8 1/2 x 11 inches. This form may also be obtained from most veterans organizations, military installations or from the National Personnel Records Center. For the latter, you may call any of the three telephone numbers listed below and leave a message with your address. A Standard Form 180 will be mailed to you.

Army	(314) 538-4261
Air Force	(314) 538-4243
Navy, Marine & Coast Guard	(314) 538-4141

Addresses on the Standard Form 180 have changed in many cases. All requests for records should be mailed to the following addresses:

Air Force

Air Force officers and enlisted personnel on active duty:

Air Force Military Personnel Center
Master Records Division
550 C. Street West, Suite 50
Randolph AFB, TX 78150-4752

Current enlisted members of the Air Force National Guard:

The Adjutant General of the appropriate state. See Chapter Four for addresses.

Air Force reserve:

Air Reserve Personnel Center
6760 East Irvington Place
Denver, CO 80280-5500

Discharged, deceased and retired Air Force:

National Personnel Records Center
9700 Page Boulevard
St. Louis, MO 63132-5100

Army

Army reserve:

U.S. Army Reserve Personnel Center
ATTN: ARPC-VS
9700 Page Boulevard
St. Louis, MO 63132-5200

Army officers on active duty:

U.S. Total Army Personnel Command
200 Stoval Street
Alexandria, VA 22332-0400

Army enlisted personnel on active duty:

U.S. Army Enlisted Records
    and Evaluation Center
8899 East 56th Street
Indianapolis, IN 46249

Army National Guard officers not on active duty:

Army National Guard Readiness Center
Arlington Hall
111 S. George Mason Drive
Arlington, VA 22204-1382

Army National Guard enlisted members not on active duty:

The Adjutant General of the appropriate state. See Chapter Four for addresses

Discharged, deceased and retired Army:

National Personnel Records Center
9700 Page Boulevard
St. Louis, MO 63132-5100

Army officers separated before July 1, 1917, and enlisted members separated before November 1, 1912:

Textual Reference Branch (NNR1)
National Archives and Records Administration
Washington, DC 20408

Coast Guard

Active Coast Guard:

Commandant (MPC-S-3)
USCG Military Personnel Command
2100 2nd Street, S.W.
Washington, DC 20593-0001

Coast Guard reserve:

> Commandant (G-RSM-3)
> USCG Reserve Records Branch
> 2100 2nd Street, S.W.
> Washington, DC 20593-0001

Discharged, deceased and retired Coast Guard:

> National Personnel Records Center
> 9700 Page Boulevard
> St. Louis, MO 63132-5100

Coast Guard officers separated before January 1, 1929 and Coast Guard enlisted personnel separated before January 1, 1915:

> Textual Reference Branch (NNR1)
> National Archives and Records Administration
> Washington, DC 20408

Marine Corps

Active, selected Marine Corps reserve or TDRL:

> Headquarters U.S. Marine Corps
> (MMSB-10)
> 2008 Elliot Road
> Quantico, VA 22134-5030

Individual Ready Reserve and Fleet Marine Corps reserve:

> USMC Reserve Support Command
> (Code MMI)
> 15303 Andrews Road
> Kansas City, MO 64174

Discharged, deceased and retired Marine Corps:

National Personnel Records Center
9700 Page Boulevard
St. Louis, MO 63132-5100

Members of the Marine Corps separated before
January 1, 1905:

Textual Reference Branch (NNR1)
National Archives and Records Administration
Washington, DC 20408

Navy

Active and reserve officers and enlisted personnel of the Navy:

Bureau of Naval Personnel
Pers-313D
2 Navy Annex
Washington, DC 20370-3130

Discharged, deceased and retired Navy:

National Personnel Records Center
9700 Page Boulevard
St. Louis, MO 63132-5100

Navy officers separated before January 1, 1903,
and enlisted members separated before January 1,
1886:

Textual Reference Branch (NNR1)
National Archives and Records Administration
Washington, DC 20408

Information to Include in SF 180

Include as much information as is known about the individual, such as service number, name and service dates, date of birth, branch of service, etc. In Section II, Paragraph 1, put "request all releasable information under Freedom of Information Act" or include this statement if your request is made in a letter. No fees are charged for Freedom of Information requests by the National Personnel Records Center. Other agencies may charge a small research and copying fee. Requests may take from four to six months to be processed. The National Personnel Records Center receives approximately 200,000 letters and requests per month.

NPRC Fire

In July 1973, a fire at the National Personnel Records Center destroyed about 80 percent of the records for Army personnel discharged between November 1, 1912 and January 1, 1960. About 75 percent of the records for Air Force personnel with surnames from Hubbard through "Z" who were discharged between September 25, 1947 and January 1, 1964 were also destroyed. Statements of service and some other information may be obtained for these individuals from final pay vouchers. Also some alternate information may be obtained from records of the state Adjutants General and state veteran service officers. Statement of Service cards may be obtained from these offices for WWI veterans. There are currently over 50 million military records at the National Personnel Records Center.

NPRC Computer Index

The service number of a former military member may be obtained from NPRC if it's in their computer index and if requested under the Freedom of Information Act. Service numbers will only be provided if there are relatively few people that match the requested name. Some older records (pre-World War I) are listed by date of birth rather than service number. The index lists most military records (names and service numbers). The computer index does not list Marine Corps, Navy and Coast Guard records obtained before 1963. Social Security numbers of individuals listed in the index will not be released.

Medical Records

A military service medical record can now be found in one of the following three retirement locations:

NPRC, if the active duty ended before the following dates:

Army	October 16, 1992
Navy	January 31, 1994
Marine Corps	May 1, 1994
Air Force	May 1, 1994

The local VA Regional Office, if the veteran had previously filed a medical claim made simultaneously with separation from active duty.

The centralized VA repository (if no previous medical claim has been filed) at:

The Department of Veterans Affairs
PO Box 150950
St Louis, MO 63115-8950

Records from the Department of Veterans Affairs

The Department of Veterans Affairs (VA) only has records for veterans who have filed claims, except as noted in the paragraph above. These records usually include identifying information about the veteran such as service number, date of birth, date of death, addresses of spouse and children (or parents), etc. Information of a genealogical nature for deceased veterans may be released to anyone if its disclosure will not be detrimental to the memory of the veteran and not prejudicial to the interest of any living person. (Some VA Regional Offices do not abide by this policy except for requests by immediate family members.) Requests should be made in writing to any VA Regional office. Call (800) 827-1000 for additional information. See Chapter Five for addresses.

Records Maintained by the National Archives

The following is a list of military computer records maintained by the National Archives. These records are available on disk or in printouts.

- Repatriated Korean Conflict Prisoners of War File
- Repatriated American Prisoners of War File (VA), World War II, Korea, Vietnam
- Korean Conflict Casualty Files
- Southeast Asia Combat Area Casualties Database
- U.S. Army Korean War Casualty File

• Casualty Information System, 1961–81

All requests for copies of records must be received in writing and be accompanied by full payment. For fee and information requirements, contact:

Center for Electronic Records (NNR2)
National Archives II
8601 Adelphi Road
College Park, MD 20740-6001
(301) 713-6630/-6640, (301) 713-6911 Fax
http://www.nara.gov/

Unit Rosters and Ship Muster Rolls

Anyone can obtain copies of a unit roster or ship muster roll (list of personnel) or organizational records by requesting them from the National Personnel Records Center, the National Archives, or the appropriate armed force. If the roster is needed to support a VA claim, there is usually no cost. You may obtain such records at a minimum cost of $8.30 (deposit) an hour plus a searching cost of $13.25 per hour if your request is for matters other than VA claims. Reunion requests receive low priority and will take more time to process. You may also make a "Freedom of Information Act Request" for a roster, in which case there is no fee charged by the National Personnel Records Center and usually a small fee by the armed forces.

If you are planning a reunion or need the service number of an individual, a roster/muster roll is the place to start. The roster/muster roll will have name, rank and service number (if prior to July 1, 1969 for Army and Air Force; July 1, 1972 for Navy and Marine Corps; and October 1, 1974 for Coast Guard) but

Social Security numbers will be removed. Be sure to state in your letter the date of the roster/muster roll requested (e.g., May 1940) and that this is a "Freedom of Information Act Request" (do not mention "reunions" on this request). The National Personnel Records Center has copies of the following:

- U.S. Army Morning Reports and Personnel rosters from November 1, 1912 to 1974 and all subsequent reports (including some SIDPERS reports) after Morning Reports were discontinued. All rosters for Army and Army Air Force units for the years 1944, 1945 and 1946 were destroyed.

- U.S. Air Force Morning Reports from September 1947 to June 30, 1966 when Morning Reports were discontinued. The Air Force did not prepare unit rosters.

- U.S. Navy Muster Rolls from 1939 through 1966 (ships only).

Many of these rosters and muster rolls are taken from microfilm and the quality can be very poor because of age or fire damage. It is advisable to request rosters for several months before and after the actual date needed. Unit rosters and ship muster rolls usually contain the names, rank and service numbers of assigned members. Prior to World War I, these usually contained name and rank only.

National Personnel Records Center
9700 Page Blvd
St. Louis, MO 63132

Army   (314) 538-4261
Air Force   (314) 538-4243
Navy, MC & Coast Guard   (314) 538-4141

Information concerning service of individuals in military organization and of civilian employees in military agencies from 1776 to 1916, Morning Reports for Army units before 1917, Staff Daily Journals, After Action Reports and Operational Reports (lessons learned) from World War II, the Korean War and the Vietnam War are available from:

Textual Reference Branch
National Archives II
8601 Adelphi Road
College Park, MD 20740-6001
(3010 713-7250, (301) 713-7482 Fax

To obtain copies of rosters of Army reserve units from 1917 to the present, contact:

Army Reserve Personnel Center
9700 Page Blvd
St. Louis, MO 63132

U.S. Navy Muster Rolls from 1967 to 1975 are available from:

Bureau of Naval Personnel (PERS-093)
Arlington Annex, Federal Building 2
Room 4531
Washington, DC 20370-5000

Muster rolls for U.S. Navy ships from 1800 to 1966 are available from the National Archives. These documents were normally prepared monthly and contain the names of enlisted men assigned to a ship or command. In some cases in the 1950s and 1960s a list of officers is included with the muster rolls. The muster rolls through 1860 are contained within bound volumes and can be copied only from microfilm. The muster rolls from 1860 through 1879 are in the form of large sheets which can be copied as oversized electrostatic copies for $1.80 per sheet. The muster rolls from 1879 through 1900 are in volumes which were compiled annually (microfilm copies only). The muster rolls from 1900 through 1939 are also in bound volumes, with each volume containing from one to several ships' muster rolls for a limited time period (microfilm copies only).

The Records of the Bureau of Naval Personnel, Record Group 24, have 16 mm positive microfilm copies of the muster rolls for U.S. Navy ships from 1940 through 1966.

Some of the rolls do include the original place of enlistment. These rolls can be reproduced only as microfilm copies for $0.33 per foot of microfilm. Paper copies are not available, nor can less than a full roll of microfilm be reproduced. A number of images may be illegible due to the poor quality of the original microfilm. The original paper muster rolls were destroyed by the Department of the Navy after filming.

The muster rolls from 1940 through 1949 are arranged so that one ship is on each roll of microfilm. After 1949, ships and shore activities were assigned activity numbers, and the muster rolls were microfilmed so that each roll contains several activities for a limited time period, usually 2 years.

Do not send any money with information requests. Each requester will be provided an order form with the appropriate information listed, to use in ordering copies. All requests for information or for copies of these records should be directed to:

Textual Reference Branch
National Archives II
8601 Adelphi Road
College Park, MD 20740-6001
(301) 713-7250, (301) 713-7482 Fax

The National Archives also has custody of deck logs of U.S. Navy ships from 1801 through June 1945. The logs from the 19th century through 1930 are in bound volumes. Officers' names usually appear on the first of each month's deck log. Only microfilm copies of such records are offered, as the process of making paper copies can permanently damage the bindings. The current fee for microfilm copies is $0.33 per image, which corresponds to a page of text.

The deck logs after 1930 can be taken apart and electrostatic (paper) copies can be made for $0.25 per page. It is estimated that most logs of this time period comprise approximately 45 pages per month, although larger ships such as battleships and carriers comprise approximately 55 pages per month. The deck logs of this time period include a monthly roster of officers which lists name of officer, rank, and his next of kin.

For information on these deck logs, contact the National Archives at the address listed above.

U.S. Navy muster rolls from 1976 to the present are available from:

Enlisted Personnel Management Center
Code 312
New Orleans, LA 70159

The Suitland Reference Branch, National Archives has custody of the deck logs from July 1945 through 1963. The deck logs from 1962 through 1978 are at the Washington National Records Center, but access to them is controlled by:

Textual Reference Branch
National Archives II
8601 Adelphi Road
College Park, MD 20740-6001
(301) 713-7250, (301) 713-7482 Fax

U.S. Marine Corps unit diaries from the Vietnam War to the present are held by the U.S. Marine Corps Headquarters. The records of the above period are not open to visiting researchers. However, interested persons may write to that office to request no more than three rosters for specific months and years.

Records Service Section
Headquarters USMC/MMSB-10
Building 2008, Room 203
Quantico, VA 22134-5002

Marine Corps After Action Reports and all unit historical records prior to 1963 are available from:

Textual Reference Branch National Archives II
8601 Adelphi Road
College Park, MD 20740-6001
(301) 713-7250, (301) 713-7482 Fax

The Reference Section of the Marine Corps Historical Center has on microfilm, muster rolls (1807 to 1949) and unit diaries (1950 to pre-Vietnam) which contain rosters. These records are arranged by month and year, and list the officers and enlisted Marines within a unit. They were either submitted at the company level of command, or the battalion/squadron level of command. The above records are open to researchers. Interested persons may write to request one muster roll or unit diary roster for a specific month and year.

Marine Corps Historical Center
Reference Section, Building 58
Washington Navy Yard
Washington, DC 20374-0580
(202) 433-3483, (202) 433-4691 Fax

U.S. Coast Guard Muster Rolls

U.S. Coast Guard muster rolls are primarily those for vessels operated by the Revenue Cutter Service which predated the establishment of the United States Coast Guard. The muster rolls are arranged alphabetically by the name of the vessel, and then chronologically, chiefly from the 1840s to about 1915. Some are a combination muster roll and payroll. The information usually shown is the name and rank of each officer on the vessel and names and ranks of enlisted men. Many entries show for enlisted men the place of birth, place of enlistment, salary information, and explanation of periods of absence during the month. Verification of the service of an enlisted man cannot be made without knowing the name of the vessel on which he served and his approximate period of service on the vessel. Most muster rolls are oversize one-page documents and are copied for $1.50 per page.

The muster rolls do not include a name index for enlisted men, but this information is available for line and engineer officers from about 1870 to the early 1900s. Muster rolls and/or payrolls up to the early 1930s for some shore units of the Coast Guard are also available. No listing exists at present showing the holdings of muster rolls for shore units.

Textual Reference Branch
National Archives II
8601 Adelphi Road
College Park, MD 20740-6001
(301) 713-7250, (301) 713-7482 Fax

U.S. Coast Guard muster rolls from 1914 to the present for vessels, districts, life boat stations, miscellaneous units, and recruiting stations are available from the above address.

Rosters for National Guard Units During WWII

Rosters of National Guard units that served on active duty during World War II, in some cases, may be obtained from the appropriate state Adjutant General's office, state military historical office, state military museum, National Guard association or from the appropriate military reunion organization. Rosters are also available from the National Personnel Records Center (except for 1944 to 1946). See Chapter Three for addresses of state Adjutant General's offices.

Unit Yearbooks and Cruise Books

Many military organizations prepare yearbooks that include pictures and rosters of individuals assigned to the unit. Additionally, most Coast Guard and Navy ships prepare cruise books. During and immediately after World War II, many units prepared yearbooks which included names and photos of members who were assigned, those who were killed in action, and those who received awards. Many yearbooks also contain group pictures of units and ships. Yearbooks and cruise books may be in the possession of military reunion groups or military historical organizations. The New York Public Library, Central Research, Fifth Avenue and 42nd Street, New York, NY 10018, has a large collection of these books. Jim Controvich, a military historian, has a large collection of Army and Air Force yearbooks (see entry further in this chapter). Turner Publishing Co. publishes re-issues of unit histories of World War II, Korean and Vietnam War units. Call (800) 788-3350 for information and catalog.

Ship Passenger Manifests

Passenger manifests are lists of names of individuals (civilian or military) who were passengers on Navy or merchant marine ships. Passenger manifests prior to 1941 are maintained by the National Archives in Washington, DC. The manifests for the period 1942–1955 were apparently destroyed. The manifests for 1956 to the present are maintained by the National Personnel Records Center. For fee and information requirements, contact:

National Archives
Seventh and Pennsylvania Avenue, N.W.
Washington, DC 20408
(202) 501-5385/5395, (202) 208-1903 Fax

or

National Personnel Records Center
Attn: Organizational Records Branch
9700 Page Boulevard
St. Louis, MO 63132-5100

Seaweed's Ship's History sells histories of all U.S. Navy, U.S. Army Transports, and most U.S. Coast Guard and Liberty ships. They have partial, up-to-date crew rosters of the ships. They also have lists of sunken U.S. ships. Lists are free with the purchase of a ship's history or $1.00 without an order. Include a self-addressed stamped envelope:

Seaweed's Ship's History
PO Box 154M
Sisterville, WV 26175
(800) 732-9333, (304) 652-1525 Phone and Fax

Military Historical Organizations

The following military historical organizations can be of great help in providing unit and ship historical information. While most cannot search for individuals, many have names of unit and ship commanders, officers' registers, key personnel and other individuals who have made significant contributions to a unit's or ship's history. These people, if living, may know the location of the person you are looking for.

These historical organizations have station lists, unit directories, and order of battle information which can assist in determining the location of a ship or unit on a particular date. They also may provide designation of the units that were assigned to a particular city on a specific date.

Air Force

Air University Historian
55 LeMay Plaza South
Maxwell AFB, AL 36112
(334) 953-5262
(334) 953-2692 Fax

Air Force Historian
60 AMW/HO
Travis AFB, CA 94535
(707) 424-3241
E-Mail:cstarr@amw
60.travis.af.mil

Air Force Historical Office
110 Luke Avenue, Suite 405
Bolling AFB, DC 20332
(202) 767-5764
(202) 767-5527 Fax

Air Force Museum
1100 Staatz Street
Building 489
W-Patt. AFB, OH 45433
(513) 255-4644
(513) 255-3910 Fax

Air Force Museum Fndtn.
PO Box 1903
W-Patt. AFB, OH 45433
(513) 258-1218
(513) 258-3816 Fax

AETC/HO
100 "H" Street, Suite 5
Randolph AFB, TX 78150
(210) 652-6564
(210) 652-4319 Fax
E-mail: manning.aetcho@
gate2.aetc.af.mil

Air Combat Command
Attn: Historian
162 Dodd Blvd., Ste 132
Langley AFB, VA 23665
(804) 764-3186
(804) 764-6088 Fax
E-mail: hccho@hqaccho.langley.af.mil

Army

The Institute/Land Warfare
AUSA
2110 Washington Blvd.
Washington, DC 20005
(800) 336-4570
(703) 243-2589 Fax
E-mail: ausahqq@aol.com

U.S. Army Center of
  Military History
1099 14th Street, N.W.
Washington, DC 20005
(202) 761-5413

U.S. Army Military
  History Institute
Bldg 22, Upton Hall
Carlisle Barracks
Carlisle, PA 17013-5008
(717) 245-3611
(717) 245-3711 Fax

Command Historian
HQ U.S. Forces Korea
8th Army
ATTN: Historian
APO, AP 96203

Coast Guard

Coast Guard Museum
U.S. Coast Guard Academy
New London, CT 06320
(203) 444-8444

Coast Guard Museum,
  Northwest
1519 Alaskan Way South
Seattle, WA 98134

Marine Corps

Marine Corps Historical Ctr
901 M Street, S.E., Bldg 58
Washington Navy Yard
Washington, DC 20374
(202) 433-3483
(202) 433-4691 Fax

National Guard

National Guard Assn Library
1 Massachusetts Ave. N.W.
Washington, DC 20001
(202) 789-0031
(202) 682-9358 Fax

National Guard Bureau
  Historical Services
Branch NGB-PAH
5109 Leesburg Pk Fwy
Falls Church, VA 22041

Navy
Navy Museum/Ship Histories
1st Floor, Bldg 57
Washington Navy Yard
901 M Street, S.E.
Washington, DC 20374

All Services
The American Legion
National Headquarters Library
PO Box 1055
Indianapolis, IN 46206
(317) 630-1366, (317) 630-1241 Fax

Base and Post Libraries

Base and Post libraries can, in many cases, provide limited information concerning units that were assigned to their particular installation. Unit histories, books about units, officers registers, morning reports, muster rolls, unit diaries and journals may be available. It is suggested you write to the individual library to request information and assistance. If you desire to contact them by telephone, call the appropriate information operator listed in Chapter Two (Base and Post locator services) to obtain the correct telephone number and hours of operation. You do not have to have a military affiliation to visit or to obtain information from these libraries.

Listed below are military libraries that have extensive collections of the military information listed above. The majority have large collections of Officers Registers of their appropriate branch. It is suggested you contact the information section of these libraries.

Military Academy Libraries

U.S. AF Academy Library
HQUSAFA/ESSEL
2354 Fairchild Drive
USAF Academy, CO 80840
(719) 472-4664
(719) 472-4754 Fax

U.S. Coast Guard
Academy Library
New London, CT 06320
(203) 444-8444

U.S. Military Academy Library
Building 757
West Point, NY 10996-1799
(914) 938-2230
(914) 938-3752 Fax

U.S. Naval Academy
Library
589 McNair Road
Annapolis, MD 21402
(410) 293-3669 Phone/Fax

Other libraries

Ft. Sam Houston Library
Building 1222
Ft. Sam Houston, TX 78234
(210) 221-4387

Library of Congress
101 Independence Ave. SE
Washington, DC 20540

Marine Corps Research
 Center Library
MC Combat Dev. Command
2040 Broadway Street
Quantico, VA 22134-5107
(703) 784-4348
(703) 784-4306 Fax

Pentagon Library
6605 Army Pentagon
Washington, DC 20310
(703) 697-4301
(703) 693-6543

U.S. Air Force NCO
 Academy Library
1110 481 Williamson Street
Maxwell AFB
Gunter Annex, AL 36114
(334) 416-3103

U.S. Army War College
 Library, AWCSL
Carlisle Barracks, PA 17013
(717) 245-3660, 245-3322 Fax

Military Magazine

Military is a monthly magazine that likes to say it "tells it like it was, and is—not like some bureaucrat would like you to think it should have been."

Published monthly, *Military* is oriented toward a readership of former service members from all services. Subscribers write the articles about their personal experiences in war and peace from World War II through Korea, Vietnam, and right up to the present. Also included each month is commentary regarding the current world situation from such military personnel as Lt. Gen. V. H. "Brute" Krulak, USMC (Ret), Col. Harry Summers, Jr., USA (Ret) and columnist Reed Irvine. Intelligence reports compiled by the staff from sources in Asia, the Americas, and Europe keep readers up-to-date on world events. A free monthly locator service, along with a list of unit reunions and military book reviews are also regular features. Subscriptions are $14 for twelve issues a year (plus $1.09 tax for California residents).

Military
2122 28th Street
Sacramento, CA 95818
(916) 457-8990

Army and Air Force Unit Histories

James T. Controvich assists individuals and associations in locating titles and reference materials concerning their units. He also prepares bibliographies concerning Army and Air Force units. He maintains the most comprehensive listing of published and printed histories available and has numerous Army and Air Force officers' registers. Using his own large library as a base, he is also familiar with the holdings of most military and institutional libraries (including unit yearbooks). For assistance, send a self-addressed stamped envelope or call after 7:00 p.m. EST. He also asks to be informed when authors or associations prepare new histories so that he can incorporate them into his bibliographic files and library. James Controvich is one of the outstanding unit historians in the United States. For additional information contact:

James T. Controvich
97 Mayfield Street
Springfield, MA 01108
(413) 734-4856

Still Photographs Created by the Military

To obtain information on photographs created by the military branches prior to 1982, contact:

Still Picture Branch
National Archives
8001 Adelphi Road
College Park, MD 20740

To obtain information for photographs created by the military branches after 1982, contact:

DOD/Still Media Records Center
Building 168
Naval Station, Anacostia
Washington, DC 20374

Records of Civil Service and Military Dependents

Complete information from the files of civil service personnel and military dependents may be obtained with the written consent of the individual (or next of kin, if deceased) or by court order.

The following information may be obtained under the Freedom of Information Act from records of most present and former federal employees:

- Name
- Present and past position titles and occupational series
- Present and past grades
- Present and past annual salary rates
- Present and past duty stations
- Position descriptions

To obtain personnel records of individuals who were employed by the Federal Civil Service, U.S. Postal Service, and medical records of dependents of active duty (Army and Air Force) and retired military personnel contact:

National Personnel Records Center
Civilian Personnel Records
111 Winnebago Street
St. Louis, MO 63118
(314) 425-5761

Medical records of Navy, Marine Corps and Coast Guard dependents are located at:

National Personnel Records Center
9700 Page Boulevard
St. Louis, MO 63132-5100
(314) 538-4141

Requests for retirement or insurance information, or medical records of civil service personnel should be sent to:

Office of Personnel Management
Compensation Group
1900 E. Street, N.W.
Washington, DC 20415

Also see "Locating Civil Service Employees" in Chapter Thirteen.

Obtain Military Information from Researcher

Colonel Paul Winkel, Jr. researches MIA/POW files at the Library of Congress and organization files at the National Archives. For additional information and fees contact:

Col. Paul Winkel, Jr., USA, (Ret)
46467 Saffron Court
Sterling, VA 20165
(703) 406-4646

Chapter 9

VERIFYING MILITARY SERVICE

Thousands of people make false claims about their military service. As a result, many people want to know how they can verify if a person is a veteran or find out exactly what a person's military credentials are.

Most of the time questions arise because the individual boldly claims to have received awards for valor or to have been assigned to special units such as the Navy Seals or the Green Berets (strange how no one ever claims to have been a clerk). Other situations involve individuals who claim to have been promoted to an unusually high rank, been involved in clandestine operations or assigned to highly classified units. But some cases only involve individuals who claim to have served in the military. The skeptical person often states that something "just does not seem right" about the individual's story.

Millions of veterans have served with valor and distinction, and few of these people brag about their accomplishments. The majority of veterans who have done extraordinary things are usually very modest or quiet about their accomplishments. It is most often the fakes who are loud mouths and braggarts.

Many of these fakes claim they were on secret missions and performed secret and special assignments. The usual story is that these missions and jobs were so highly classified that there is no record of them and cannot be verified.

The television program "60 Minutes" aired a segment on this problem. They cited a case where a WWII Navy vet claimed he had earned the Medal of Honor. When he was interviewed on the show, he seemed to be telling the truth. However, a thorough investigation by "60 Minutes" proved he was never awarded the nation's highest honor.

Some individuals have falsely claimed they were prisoners of war which is one of the ugliest claims one can make considering the suffering real POWs have experienced.

Why do apparently reasonable people make such false or exaggerated claims? Many do this to impress their girlfriend, family, friends, co-workers or members of a veterans organization. Others do it to get VA benefits, such as disability compensation, education benefits, medical treatment in VA hospitals, and admission to VA nursing homes. Some make false claims about their service to obtain civil service job preference (state and federal). Others do it to get personalized license plates available to Purple Heart recipients. One person posed as a veteran so he could be buried in a National Cemetery.

The question is where can information be obtained to check out these phonies and expose them as fakes? All of the addresses and phone numbers you will need are in this book. No matter what the claim is, you can normally verify it yourself. There is some information that cannot be obtained from military records because of national security reasons, but these cases are few and far between. Some information can be obtained simply by calling the Department of Veterans Affairs (VA) at (800) 827-1000. The primary source of information from the federal government is the National Personnel Records Center. Other major sources are the National Archives, Armed Forces World-Wide and Base Locators, military historical offices, military historical libraries, casualty offices, public affairs offices, state veterans affairs offices and state Adjutant General's offices. State and local governments, county courthouses and libraries are also important sources. Other sources of information include family history libraries, veterans organizations (national and local), historical organizations, military reunion groups, and computer locator companies.

The most complete and accurate way to verify military service is to request a copy of the person's records (if there are any) from the National Personnel Records Center. You can obtain these under the Freedom of Information Act. They will show the individual's rank, service dates, places served, units assigned, awards, decorations and promotions that were received (if any), education levels, if they were ever court-martialed, any overseas service dates, and names of dependents. If the individual is applying for a job, the employer can request that he or she sign a request for records, and the entire military personnel and medical records will be sent to the employer. Also, if there is a court case, the entire records can be obtained by an attorney if a court order is signed by a judge.

You will need the authorization of the individual to obtain a Report of Separation (DD 214). This is done frequently by employers and some veteran organizations.

You can also obtain unit rosters, ships muster rolls, morning reports, daily journals, after action reports, unit histories, yearbooks, cruise books, ships logs, order of battle information, and troop lists to help you in the verification process. You can verify the names of unit commanders and other key personnel from these reports or you can verify their names in officers' registers. These books can also be used to verify that an individual was actually an officer (see Chapters Five and Eight).

Before you begin any search for information it is best to have the person's legal name, service number and/or Social Security number. The date of birth will also be helpful. If the person claims he is currently on active duty in a branch of the armed forces, you can contact the appropriate World-Wide Locator to determine if the person is on active duty (see Chapter Two).

If he claims he is retired or in one of the reserve components, then contact the appropriate locator. You can also call the Retired Pay center to verify that the person is receiving retired pay (see Chapters Two and Four).

If he claims he is a veteran (and not in the reserves or retired) there are several things that can be done. Call the VA and find out if they have a file on him. Not everyone who is a veteran is in the VA file. Prior to 1974, only those veterans who applied for benefits of any kind were put into the file. But starting in 1974 and continuing on today, the VA lists everyone who separated or retired from the service. This is true even if the individual did not make a claim. Therefore, you should be able to verify branch of service and service dates.

You can also check with reunion organizations and veterans organizations. But be careful as these organizations do not usually ask for proof of service to join. Many organizations require a copy of the individual's DD 214 before accepting him or her as a member, but these documents are often altered or forged. If you know the county where he lived after he was discharged, check with the county courthouse and find out if he registered his discharge. You can obtain a copy. State Veteran Affairs offices can also provide discharges in some cases.

Perhaps one of the best ways to verify a person's claim about military service is by contacting people who served in the unit he claims to have been in. This can be done easily if there is a reunion group of the unit. Check with VETS and The National Reunion Registry (see Chapter Seven).

If you have determined that a person is fabricating information about his or her military service, you should present this information to the appropriate official or the person who initially requested it. It is not recommended that you confront the impostor with this information first. It is against federal law to alter or counterfeit a Report of Separation (DD 214).

It is also against federal law to lie about military service when applying for federal benefits or seeking veteran preference for federal civil service hiring. Serious cases of fraud should be reported to the FBI. Frauds should be exposed. It is an insult to the millions of veterans who served their country honorably to do otherwise.

Following is a list of organizations that may assist in determining if someone has been a Navy Seal, in the Army Special Forces or Special Operations:

UDT/Seal Museum   (407) 595-1570
3300 A1A
Ft. Pierce, FL 34949

They have a database of people who have completed Seal training.

Radix Press   (713) 683-9076
Steve Sherman   (713) 683-8314 Fax
2314 Chesire Lane
Houston, TX 77018

Has names of Special Forces members who served in Southeast Asia. (He is searching for further copies of orders, awards and other documents relating to Special Forces in Vietnam).

Special Forces Association
PO Box 41436
Fayetteville, NC 28309-1436

Special Operations Association
5130 E. Charleston Blvd, Suite 5-583F
Las Vegas, NV 89122

Also check *Medal of Honor Recipients 1863–1994, Vols. I & II.* Compiled by George Lang, Raymond L. Collins and Gerald White.

Chapter 10

DETERMINING IF A VETERAN IS DECEASED

This chapter provides addresses of government and private organizations that may be able to tell you if the person you are looking for is deceased. It also explains how to obtain official military casualty reports and how to find out where a military veteran is buried.

Using the Social Security Administration

The Social Security Administration will tell you if they have a report that an individual is deceased, if you provide them with a SSN or a name and date of birth. It is also helpful if you have the names of the parents of the individual. Call the SSA at (800) 772-1213.

Using the Department of Veterans Affairs

The VA will tell you if a veteran is deceased if they can identify him in their files. They will also give you his date of death and place of burial, if known. The VA is informed of veteran's deaths by funeral homes, family members and other government agencies and have excellent records in this regard. Call any VA regional office for assistance (see Chapter Five for additional details and telephone numbers).

Locating Next of Kin of Military Casualties

You may write to the appropriate armed service for assistance if you wish to contact the next of kin of military members who were casualties during recent wars. Names and addresses of next of kin are contained on all casualty reports. Casualty information normally is made only through written request, and casualty reports are for release primarily to the next of kin. Any reports that are released to other parties under the Freedom of Information Act are normally sanitized, i.e., next of kin information is deleted.

Casualty records cover 1942 to present (Marine Corps) and World War II to present (Navy), and contain names and service numbers of personnel who are deceased or missing and those injured in a battle zone.

Headquarters, U.S. Marine Corps
Casualty Branch MHP-10
Washington, DC 20380-0001
(703) 696-2069, (703) 696-2072 Fax

HQ AFMPC/DPMCB
550 C. Street West, Room A315
Randolph AFB, TX 78150-6001
(210) 652-5513

Bureau of Naval Personnel, BNP-633
Casualty Assistance Branch
Washington, DC 20370-5663
(703) 614-2926, (703) 325-5300 Fax
(800) 443-9297

The U.S. Army Mortuary Affairs and Casualty Support Division has access to individual deceased personnel records for Americans who died overseas during World War II and the Korean War. They have access to individual deceased personnel records for Army members only who died in Southeast Asia during the Vietnam War.

The files contain information pertaining to the disposal of remains including place of death and place of burial. The files do not contain information pertaining to awards and decorations.

Director, Army Casualty and Memorial
    Affairs Operation Center
Total Army Personnel Command, DAPC-PED
2461 Eisenhower Avenue
Alexandria, VA 22331-0482
(703) 325-5300

Locating Grave Sites of U.S. Servicemen Buried Overseas

The American Battle Monuments Commission (ABMC) can provide names of 124,914 U.S. war dead of World War I and II who are interned in American burial grounds in foreign countries. The ABMC also can provide the names of any 94,093 U.S. servicemen and women who were missing in action or lost or buried at sea during the World Wars, the Korean and Vietnam Wars. For further information contact:

American Battle Monuments Commission
Casemir Pulaski Building
20 Massachusetts Avenue, N.W.
Washington, DC 20314-0300
(202) 761-0537, (202) 761-0533
(202) 761-1375 Fax

Locating Grave Sites of Veterans and Their Dependents Buried in VA Cemeteries

The National Cemetery System (NCS), Department of Veterans Affairs, provides limited genealogy services and burial location assistance to the next of kin or close friends of decedents.

NCS personnel can research records to determine if a specific decedent is interred in one of the VA National Cemeteries. However, all requests must relate to individuals since research cannot be conducted on groups. To request a burial search on a specific individual, it is requested that the following information be provided:

- full name (first, middle, and last)
- date and place of birth
- date and place of death
- state at which entered military service
- rank and military unit in which served on active duty

No form is required and no fee is charged for this service. Simply provide the above information in a letter addressed to:

Director for Technical Support (401B)
National Cemetery System
Department of Veterans Affairs
810 Vermont Avenue, N.W.
Washington, DC 20420
(202) 273-5226, (202) 273-6697 Fax

Military Casualty Reports

Korean Conflict Casualty File. Contains data of all U.S. Military personnel who died by hostile means as a result of combat duty in the Korean conflict. There are 32,642 records with dates of death from 1950–57.

Southeast Asia Combat Area Casualties Database. Contains 58,152 records of all U.S. Military personnel who died as a result of hostilities or other causes in Cambodia, China, Laos, North Vietnam, South Vietnam or Thailand from 1957–89.

Korean War Casualty File—U.S. Army. Contains 109,975 records of both fatal and non-fatal Army casualties.

The Casualty Information System. Contains records of casualties suffered by all U.S. Army personnel and their dependents from 1961–81. Extracts of records for all U.S. Army active duty personnel who have died are available.

For fee and information requirements on any of the above, contact:

Center for Electronic Records (NSX)
National Archives and Records Administration
8601 Adelphi Road
College Park, MD 20740-6001
(301) 713-6630

World War II Army Air Force Accident Reports

World War II Army Air Force and other USAF Accident Reports are in the custody of:

HQ USAF Safety Agency
AFSA/IMR
9700 Avenue G, S.E.
Kirtland AFB, NM 87117-5670

Locating Children of World War II Casualties

The American World War II Orphans Network is a network of sons and daughters of World War II casualties and an orphan registry. At present, they have over 800 orphans in their database. They provide a locator service to help orphans, war buddies, and family members find each other. They also provide information on locating deceased veterans' government records and other public records, publish a newsletter with information about finding records, and discuss issues pertinent to their members. They share information and help one another in any way they can. They have a goal of locating all World War II orphans and to locate all U.S. memorials which list the names of World War II casualties. This is a non-profit organization. Entry into the database is free. Self-addressed stamped envelopes are appreciated when making inquiries.

American World War II Orphans Network
PO Box 4369
Bellingham, WA 98227
(360) 733-1678, (360) 715-8180 Fax
E-mail: awon@aol.com

Locating Families and Friends of Deceased Vietnam Veterans

"In Touch" is a locator service whose main goal is to connect Vietnam veterans with the families of those who died in Vietnam.

Under the "In Touch" program, support networks for Sons and Daughters In Touch and Siblings In Touch connect family members who benefit from communicating with each other.

In cooperation with other locator services, "In Touch" also helps Vietnam veterans find each other. There is no charge for any of the "In Touch" services which are sponsored by Friends of the Vietnam Veterans Memorial.

This organization also has a copy of the Vietnam casualty file (those listed on The Wall).

Friends of Vietnam Veterans Memorial
2030 Clarendon Boulevard, Suite 412
Arlington, VA 22201
(703) 525-1107
E-mail: 71035,3126@compuserve.com

Chapter 11

FAMILY HISTORY INFORMATION FOR VETERANS

This chapter describes various methods of searching for genealogical information on veterans.

To do thorough genealogical research for a family history of a person who was in the armed forces, the following steps are recommended. These are in addition to normal genealogical research conducted for a family history. The assistance of a genealogist who specializes in military records may save you a great deal of time.

- Determine if the individual is listed in the separate military schedule of the national census of 1890 (Union veterans), 1900, 1910 and 1920, if appropriate.

- Obtain copies of the individual's induction (draft) records, Statement of Service card (WWI), military personnel and medical records. If the individual served in more than one branch of the service, separate requests must be made as the records are not combined. For additional information, see Chapter Eight.

- Obtain copies of pension records in the federal and state archives and all records held by the Department of Veterans Affairs. See Chapter Eight.

- If the individual ever served as an officer, obtain copies of entries in *Officers Registers* for each year that he or she served as an officer. The entries usually give information on promotion dates, civilian and military schools attended and awards and decorations received. See the library section in Chapter Eight.

- Obtain copies of unit histories of all units in which the individual served. Obtain unit and individual photos from National Archives. See Chapter Eight.

- Obtain appropriate copies of unit rosters, muster rolls, after action reports, daily staff journals, deck logs, morning reports, and daily journals for all units and ships the individual was assigned to. See Chapter Eight.

- If the individual was wounded or killed while in the service, attempt to obtain copies of casualty reports, if those reports were not in their official military personnel records. See Chapter Ten.

- If the individual was a Prisoner of War, obtain copies or excerpts from databases and records retained by the National Archives. See Chapter Eight.

- Obtain records of membership in veteran, military and patriotic organizations as well as military unit reunion organizations. See Chapter Five.

- Apply for medals and awards that the individual earned but may not have received. Write to the National Personnel Records Center for additional information. See Chapter Eight.

- Obtain copies of membership records, yearbooks, cruise books, newspapers, etc., in military fraternal organizations, military colleges and high school alumni associations. Also, obtain records of churches on or near military bases to which he may have belonged. See Chapters Eight and Thirteen.

- Obtain a copy of the individual's obituary. Research military newspaper files for articles about the individual. See Chapters Eight and Thirteen.

- Determine location of burial site in military cemeteries, national (VA) cemeteries, or overseas American burial grounds. See Chapter Ten.

Chapter 12

SOCIAL SECURITY NUMBERS AND SERVICE NUMBERS

This chapter provides information concerning military service numbers and Social Security numbers. Both of these numbers can be used to obtain the former and current locations of an individual.

Service Numbers

Service numbers were first issued (for enlisted men in the Army) on February 28, 1918. Army officer service numbers were not issued until 1921. Prior to this, the name of the individual was the only means of identification.

Regular Army service numbers ranged from 1 through 19,999,999 (8 numerical digits not including any letter prefix or suffix, see Chart Five) until July 1, 1969, when Social Security numbers became the identifying number. The Air Force shared numbers after its establishment on Sept. 25, 1947, until July 1, 1969, when it began using Social Security numbers.

During the period 1918 through 1939, Army enlisted service numbers were assigned at random without regard to any geographical area.

Beginning in 1940 each entrance and examining station in the U.S. was allocated certain sets of service numbers for enlisted Army personnel. In most cases, not all of these numbers were used because of an overestimate of needs in particular areas.

The U.S. was divided into six Service areas which were later changed to Army areas. A set of numbers was allocated to each entrance station identified with that Army area. For example, First Army: 11 million through 12 million and 31 million through 32 million and 51 million through 51,999,999; Second Army: 13 million through 15 million and 52 million through 52,999,999 also 33 and 35 million numbers; Third Army: 14 million through 34 million and 53 million; Fourth Army: 18 million through 38 million and 54 million; Fifth Army: 16 million through 17 million and 36 million through 37 million and 55 million; Sixth Army: 19 million through 39 million and 56 million.

Numbers starting with 10 million and 50 million were assigned to members who entered the service outside the Continental U.S. Numbers starting with 20 million were assigned to members of the National Guard on active duty (1940–1946). Numbers 21 million through 29 million were assigned to members of the National Guard (1946–1969) (see Chart Three).

Numbers starting with 30 million were assigned to those men who were inducted (drafted) during World War II (1940–1946). Forty-two through 46 million were assigned to members inducted between

1943–1946. Numbers in the 50 million series were assigned to those who were inducted in the Korean and Vietnam wars (1948–1966).

Also, some 57 million numbers were issued during the Vietnam war. Numbers starting with 60 million were assigned to Army and Air Force enlisted men from 1966–1969. Numbers starting with 90 million (approximately 20,000) were assigned to members of the Philippine Army during World War II. Forty and 41 million numbers, 47 through 49 million and 70 through 89 million numbers were not allocated.

Army officer's service numbers never exceeded seven numerical digits plus letter prefix for non-regular officers and six numerical digits plus letter prefix for regular officers (1919 through 1969). See Chart Five for explanation of prefixes and suffixes to service numbers.

The Navy, Marine Corps and Coast Guard began using service numbers in 1918 for enlisted members. These consisted of different sets of numbers ranging from one digit numbers to seven digit numbers and had no significance as to where they were issued. Blocks of numbers were assigned to recruiting offices throughout the world and to some headquarters activities. Navy officer service numbers were called file numbers. These branches of the service also assigned service number to the files of former members who had served prior to the time when service numbers were used.

The Department of Veterans Affairs and the National Personnel Records Center use only the numerical portion of the service number in their indexes and databases. No letter prefixes or suffixes are used.

Using Charts One, Two and Three

To determine where and when a Regular (10 through 19 million) Army or Air Force service number was assigned:

- Determine in what state the service number was issued. See Chart One.
- Determine on what date the service number was issued. See Chart Two.

Example: 12,250,000 was issued in Delaware or New Jersey and was issued between 1946 and 1948.

To determine where and when a draftee service number (30–39 million and 50–57 million) was issued:

- Determine in what state the service number was issued. See Chart One.
- Notice that 31–37 million service numbers were assigned between 1940 and 1946; 51 and 57 million service numbers were assigned between 1948 and 1969.

Example: A service number 38,945,340 was issued in Texas, Louisiana, Oklahoma or New Mexico between 1940 and 1946. Service numbers beginning with 50 were assigned in Alaska, Hawaii, Panama, and Puerto Rico between 1948–69.

To determine where and when a National Guard service number was assigned:

- Determine to which state the service number was assigned. See Chart Three.
- Service numbers were utilized from 1946–69.

Chart One

Service Numbers, First Two Numbers

The numbers below are the first two numbers of the eight digit service numbers. These service numbers were assigned by entrance stations in the states indicated to Air Force and Army enlisted male personnel.

(1) Name of state or territory
(2) Regular and reserve Air Force and Army
(3) Draftees 1940–1946
(4) Draftees 1948–1969

(1)	(2)	(3)	(4)	(1)	(2)	(3)	(4)
AL	14	34	53	NV	19	39	56
AK	19	39	50	NH	11	31	51
AZ	19	39	56	NJ	12	32	51
AR	18	38	54	NM	18	38	54
CA	19	39	56	NY	12	32	51
CO	17	37	55	NC	14	34	53
CT	11	31	51	ND	17	37	55
DE	12	32	51	OH	15	35	52
FL	14	34	53	OK	18	38	54
ID	19	39	56	OR	19	39	56
GA	14	34	53	PA	13	33	52
IL	16	36	55	RI	11	31	51
IN	15	35	52	SC	14	34	53
IA	17	37	55	SD	17	37	55
KS	17	37	55	TN	14	34	53
KY	15	35	52	TX	18	38	54
LA	18	38	54	UT	19	39	56
ME	11	31	51	VT	11	31	51
MD	13	33	52	VA	13	33	52
MA	11	31	51	WV	15	35	52
MI	16	36	55	WA	19	39	56

MN	.17	37	55	WI	16	36	55
MS	14	34	53	WY	17	37	55
MO	17	37	55	HI	10	30	50
MT	19	39	56	Panama	10	30	50
NE	17	37	55	PR	10	30	50

Chart Two

Regular Army and Air Force Service Numbers

Service numbers 10,000,000 through 19,999,999 were issued to Regular Air Force and Regular Army enlisted men for periods indicated below. These numbers were also assigned to enlisted male reservists.

10,000,000–10,999,999	1940–69		
11,000,000–11,142,500	1940–45	12,000,000–12,242,000	1940–45
11,142,501–11,188,000	1946–48	12,242,001–12,321,000	1946–48
11,166,001–11,238,500	1949–51	12,321,001–12,393,500	1949–51
11,238,501–11,283,000	1952–54	12,393,501–12,469,000	1952–54
11,283,001–11,344,500	1955–57	12,469,001–12,553,375	1955–57
11,344,501–11,384,000	1958–60	12,553,376–12,614,900	1958–60
11,384,001–11,999,999	1961–69	12,614,901–12,999,999	1961–69
13,000,000–13,197,500	1940–45	14,000,000–14,204,500	1940–45
13,197,501–13,299,700	1946–48	14,204,501–14,300,770	1946–48
13,299,701–13,408,700	1949–51	14,300,771–14,454,000	1949–51
13,408,701–13,511,500	1952–54	14,454,001–14,547,500	1952–54
13,511,501–13,621,140	1955–57	14,547,501–14,661,000	1955–57
13,621,141–13,705,500	1958–60	14,661,001–14,745,000	1958–60
13,705,501–13,999,999	1961–69	14,745,001–14,999,999	1961–69
15,000,000–15,201,000	1940–45	16,000,000–16,201,500	1940–45
15,201,001–15,280,500	1946–48	16,201,501–16,307000	1946–48
15,280,501–15,465,760	1949–51	16,307,001–16,398,890	1949–51
15,465,761–15,530,600	1952–54	16,398,891–16,481,925	1952–54
15,530,601–15,593,615	1955–57	16,481,926–16,600,497	1955–57
15,593,616–15,639,615	1958–60	16,600,498–16,683,100	1958–60
15,639,616–15,999,999	1961–69	16,683,101–16,999,999	1961–69

17,000,000–17,183,500	1940–45	18,546,001–18,607,725	1958–60
17,183,501–17,254,500	1946–48	18,607,726–18,999,999	1961–69
17,254,501–17,338,840	1949–51	19,000,000–19,235,500	1940–45
17,338,841–17,410,300	1952–54	19,235,501–19,324,485	1946–48
17,410,301–17,512,785	1955–57	19,324,486–19,420,000	1949–51
17,512,786–17,592,940	1958–60	19,420,001–19,520,770	1952–54
17,592,941–17,999,999	1961–69	19,520,771–19,590,665	1955–57
18,000,000–18,247,100	1940–45	19,590,666–19,597,661	1958
18,247,101–18,360,800	1946	19,597,662–19,999,999	1959–69
18,360,801–18,546,000	1947–57		

Numbers 10,000–10,999,999 were used for initial enlistments occurring outside the continental limits: Alaska, Hawaii, Puerto Rico and Panama.

Chart Three

National Guard Service Numbers

Service numbers 21,000,000 through 29,999,999 were issued to National Guard enlisted men in these states from 1946 to 1969.

First Army		**Second Army**	
CT	21,000,000–21,139,999	DE	21,140,000–21,189,999
ME	21,190,000–21,259,999	VT	22,860,000–22,909,999
MA	21,260,000–21,619,999	DC	22,910,000–22,959,999
NH	21,620,000–21,689,999	IN	22,960,000–23,169,999
NJ	21,690,000–21,899,999	KY	23,170,000–23,269,999
NY	21,900,000–22,699,999	MD	23,270,000–23,379,999
NJ	22,700,000–22,789,999	OH	23,380,000–23,729,999
RI	22,790,000–22,859,999	PA	23,730,000–24,259,999
VA	24,260,000–24,409,999	WV	24,410,000–24,479,999

Third Army

AL	24,480,000–24,619,999
FL	24,620,000–24,729,999
GA	24,730,000–24,879,999
MS	24,880,000–24,959,999
NC	24,960,000–25,109,999
SC	25,110,000–25,249,999

Fourth Army

AR	25,410,000–25,499,999
LA	25,500,000–25,629,999
NM	25,630,000–25,679,999
OK	25,680,000–25,839,999
TX	25,840,000–26,239,999
TN	25,250,000–25,409,999

Fifth Army

CO	26,240,000–26,329,999
IL	26,330,000–26,799,999
IA	26,780,000–26,919,999
KS	26,920,000–27,009,999
MI	27,010,000–27,339,999
MN	27,340,000–27,499,999
MO	27,500,000–27,659,999
NE	27,660,000–27,729,999
ND	27,730,000–27,789,999
SD	27,790,000–27,849,999
WI	27,850,000–28,019,999
WY	28,020,000–28,039,999

Sixth Army

AZ	28,040,000–28,089,999
CA	28,090,000–28,639,999
ID	28,640,000–28,709,999
MT	28,710,000–28,759,999
NV	28,760,000–28,769,999
OR	28,770,000–28,909,999
UT	28,910,000–28,969,999
WA	28,970,000–29,029,999
HI	29,030,000–29,119,999
PR	29,120,000–29,239,999
AK	29,240,000–29,249,999

Service numbers 20,000,000 to 20,999,999 were assigned to National Guard enlisted men between 1940 and 1946.

Chart Four

Dates Service Numbers were Issued

Officers	Enlisted Personnel

Air Force

1–	99,999	1947–68			
1,800,000–	1,999,999	1947–68			
2,200,000–	3,999,999	1947–68			

USAF shared enlisted SN with Army from 1947–69.

Army

1–	19,999	1921–35	1–	5,999,999	1918–19
20,000–	99,999	1935–64	6,000,000–	7,999,999	1919–40

Officers   Enlisted Personnel

Army (cont.)

Officers		Enlisted Personnel	
100,000– 124,999	P1965–69	8,000,000–8,599,999	W1948–68
100,000– 449,999	1921–41	10,000,000–19,999,999	1940–69
500,000– 2,899,999	1942–54	20,000,000–29,249,999	1940–69
3,000,000– 5,999,999	1957–68	30,000,000–39,999,999	1940–46
42,000,000–46,999,999	1943–46	50,000,000–59,999,999	1948–69
60,000,000–69,000,000	1966–69	90,000,000–90,200,000	1940–45

Coast Guard

Officers		Enlisted Personnel	
1,000– 99,999	?-74	100,000– 199,000	1915–30
		200,000– 254,000	1930–42
		255,000– 349,999	1945–62
		350,000– 499,999	1962
		500,000– 707,999	1941–45
		2,000,000– 2,199,999	1948
		3,000,000– 3,081,999	1942–44
		4,000,000– 4,040,999	1942–45
		5,000,000– 5,001,499	1942
		6,000,000– 6,207,999	1941–45
		7,000,000– 7,207,999	1943–45

Marine Corps

1,000,000– 1,697,999	1944–57
1,700,000– 1,799,999	W1942–72
1,800,000– 1,896,265	1956–60
1,896,266– 1,999,999	1956–65
2,000,000– 2,197,999	1964–72

Navy

Officers		Enlisted Personnel	
501– 124,999	1903–1941	100,000– 999,999	P1965–74
125,000– 199,999	1942	1,000,000– 1,999,999	1885–18
200,000– 254,999	1942–43		
2,000,000–9,999,999	1918–65		
255,000– 349,999	1943–44		
350,499– –499,999	1944–47		
500,000– 599,999	1947–55		
600,000– 670,899	1955–63		
670,900– 699,999	1963–65		
700,000– 707,999	1965–66	W-women	
708,000– 799,999	1966–72	P-used with prefix	

Chart Five

Service Number Prefixes and Suffixes

The majority of prefixes and suffixes were letters used with Air Force and Army service numbers. None are known to have been used with Coast Guard service numbers. The Marine Corps used "O" to denote officer and "W" for enlisted women. The Navy also used "W" for enlisted women. From December 1965 Navy enlisted personnel received six digit numbers with a "B" prefix (B100000 thru B999999). Following the "B" series was the "D" series (D100000 thru D999999). EM and EW are used to show enlisted men and enlisted women.

P—Prefix; S—Suffix; A—Army; AF—Air Force; N—Navy; MC—Marine Corps.

Letter	Use	Service	Designation
A	P	A	Enlisted women (WAC) without specification of component.
A	S	AF	Used until 1965 for Regular AF male officers.
AA	P	AF	Women enlisted personnel (WAF)
AD	P	AF	Aviation cadets.
AF	P	AF	Male enlisted personnel other than aviation cadets.
AH	P	AF	Male enlisted reserve 1962–65.
AO	P	AF	Reserve officers from about 1947–65.
AR	P	AF	Used until about 1965 for enlisted AF reserve and AF dietitians.
AW	P	AF	Used from about 1947 to 1965 for male reserve of the AF and SAF warrant officers.

E	S	AF	Used until 1965 for Regular AF male warrant officers.
ER	P	A	Members of Army Reserve, including those enlisted personnel of Army National Guard transferred from AUS, RA, or NGUS.
F	P	A	Used for field clerks in 800,000 series in WWI.
FG	P	AF	Air National Guard officers and warrant officers (male and female).
FR	P	AF	Regular AF officers and warrant officers (male and female).
FR	P	A	Certain Army enlisted reservists from date unknown through October 3, 1962.
FT	P	AF	Officers and warrant officers without component (male and female).
FV	P	AF	Reserve and warrant officers.
H	P	AF	Used until 1965 for Regular AF female warrant officers.
K	S	AF	Used until about 1965 for AF Academy cadets.
K	P	A	Female officers except Regular Army with SNs 100,001 or higher, Army Nurse Corps, Army Medical Specialists Corps, and Women's Army Corps.
KF	P	A	Regular Army women officers with SN 100,001 and higher.
L	P	A	Women's Army Corps (officers).

MJ	P	A	Occupational Therapy officers.
MM	P	A	Physical Therapy officers.
MN	P	A	Male officers of Army Nurse Corps.
MR	P	A	Dietitians.
N	P	A	Female nurses (officers).
NG	P	A	Army National Guard enlisted.
O	P	A	Male officers except Regular Army with SNs 100,001 and higher after Oct 28, 1963; Army Nurse Corps; Army Medical Specialists Corps.
O	P	MC	Marine Corps officers.
OF	P	A	Regular Army male officers with SNs 100,001 and higher after October 28, 1963.
R	P	A	Officer dietitians.
R	P	A	Used on Army WWI EM numbers 1 thru 5,999,999 if individual re-enlisted.
RA	P	A	Regular Army enlisted personnel (used since approx. Oct 1945).
RM	P	A	Regular Army EM holding appointments as warrant officers in the active Army reserve.
RO	P	A	Regular Army enlisted holding commissions in the active Army reserve.
RP	P	A	Retired EM recalled to active duty now on retired status (used only for those transferred to retired Army reserve).

RV	P	A	Women's Army Corps warrant officers holding commissions in active reserves.
RW	P	A	Warrant officers holding commissions in active reserves.
T	P	A	Flight officers appointed from enlisted ranks. Numbers range from T10,000 thru T223,600 (1942 to date unknown).
UR	P	A	Inductees holding commissions or warrants in active Army reserve.
US	P	A	Enlisted men without specification of component.
V	P	A	Women's Army Corps officers.
W	P	A	Warrant officers.
W	P	MC	Women enlisted personnel.
W	S	AF	Used until 1965 for Regular AF women commissioned officers.
W	S	N	Women enlisted personal.
WA	P	A	Regular Army enlisted women (WAC).
WL	P	A	Regular Army enlisted women holding commissions in the active Army reserve.
WM	P	A	Regular Army enlisted women holding warrants in the Army active reserve.
WR	P	A	Enlisted women reservists (WAC).

Social Security Numbers

The Social Security number (SSN) is the most important item other than the name of the individual you are trying to locate. Every member of the military, active, reserve, National Guard or retired is identified and listed by his SSN. The same is true for veterans though they can also be listed by their VA claim number or their former service number by the Department of Veterans Affairs. Service numbers were discontinued and were replaced by Social Security numbers on the following dates:

Army and Air Force	July 1, 1969
Navy and Marine Corps	July 1, 1972
Coast Guard	Oct. 1, 1974

Records in the National Personnel Records Center are identified by Social Security number except for records received before the SSN replaced the service number, in which case the service numbers are used. A few records for individuals who served prior to World War I are listed by date of birth. Most individuals who were separated from active duty were transferred to the reserves. Their records were sent to the NPRC when they were discharged from the reserves. Even if they served with a service number their records may be under their Social Security number.

There are several ways you may find a SSN. It is contained on military orders, discharges (DD 214), officers' commissions, and in the Register of Officers published by each military service from 1970 to 1976. Many bank statements contain it as well as some driver licenses and canceled checks. Personal letters from military members usually have their SSN included with the return address. All VA claim numbers issued after June 1974 included the veteran's SSN preceded by the letter "C" (example, C123456789).

You can look at old investments such as money market funds, mutual funds and stock certificates for a SSN. Most department stores ask for a person's SSN when charge accounts are opened. You might get it from schools or places of civilian employment. A SSN can, in some case, be obtained from voter registration information. Many states have DD 214 forms (discharge) recorded in county courthouses; many of these discharges contain SSNs. A SSN can also be obtained by several computer searches. *The Privacy Act of 1974 prohibits military and federal agencies from giving out a Social Security number.*

You may need the SSN to have your letters forwarded by the military, Social Security Administration or the Department of Veterans Affairs. You may also be asked for the SSN when you call an installation locator (see Base/Post Locators in Chapter Two), especially if there is more than one person with the same name. Many times individuals are listed by their SSNs because it is easier and quicker to find a number on computer records than trying to find the person by name.

Social Security Number Allocations

The Social Security Administration (SSA) was formed in 1933. Between 1933 and 1972 SSNs were assigned at field offices in each state. The area number (see below) identified the state in which the field office was located. Since 1973, SSNs have been issued by the SSA central office.

The Social Security number consists of nine digits. The first three digits are the area number. The middle two digits are the group number. The last four digits are the serial number. (Do not confuse this with the military service numbers.)

EXAMPLE: 123-45-6789

123   45   6789

Area# Group# Serial#

The *area number* assigned by the central office identifies the state indicated in the application.

The chart below shows the first 3 digits (area number) of the Social Security numbers allocated to each state and U.S. possession.

001-003. . . . . New Hampshire
004-007 . . . . Maine
008-009 . . . . Vermont
010-034. . . . . Massachusetts
035-039 . . . . Rhode Island
040-049 . . . . Connecticut
050-134 . . . . New York
135-158. . . . . New Jersey
159-211. . . . . Pennsylvania
212-220 . . . . Maryland
221-222 . . . . Delaware
223-231, 691-699*. . . . . . . Virginia
232-236 . . . . West Virginia
232, 237-246, 681-690* . . . North Carolina
247-251, 654-658* . . . . South Carolina
252-260, 667-675* . . . . Georgia
261-267, 589-595 . . . . Florida
268-302 . . . . Ohio

303–317 . . . . Indiana
318–361. . . . . Illinois
362–386 . . . . Michigan
387–399 . . . . Wisconsin
400–407 . . . . Kentucky
408–415, 756–763* . . . . Tennessee
416–424 . . . . Alabama
425–428, 587, 588*,
  752–755* . . . . Mississippi
429–432, 676–679* . . . . Arkansas
433–439, 659–665* . . . . Louisiana
440–448 . . . . Oklahoma
449–467, 627–645. . . . . Texas
468–477 . . . . Minnesota
478–485 . . . . Iowa
486–500 . . . . Missouri
501–502 . . . . North Dakota
503–504 . . . . South Dakota
505–508 . . . . Nebraska
509–515. . . . . Kansas
516–517. . . . . Montana
518–519. . . . . Idaho
520 . . . . Wyoming
521–524, 650–653* . . . . Colorado
525, 585, 648–649* . . . . New Mexico
526–527, 600–601 . . . . Arizona
528–529, 646–647* . . . . Utah
530, 680*. . . . . Nevada
531– 539. . . . . Washington
540–544 . . . . Oregon
545–573, 602–626* . . . . California
574 . . . . Alaska
575–576, 750–751* . . . . Hawaii
577–579 . . . . District of Columbia

580 . . . . Virgin Islands
580–584, 596–599 . . . . Puerto Rico
586 . . . . Guam
586 . . . . American Samoa
586 . . . . Philippine Islands
700–728** . . . . Railroad Board

*Allocated but not yet issued.

**RRB (Railroad Board). Issuance of these numbers to railroad employees was discontinued July 1, 1963.

Note: The same area number shown more than once means that certain numbers have been transferred from one state to another, or that an area number has been divided for use among certain geographic locations.

Area numbers range from 001 through 587, 589 through 649, and 700 through 728. Social Security numbers containing area numbers other than these are invalid.

After converting from service numbers to Social Security numbers as a means of identification, the military assigned dummy Social Security numbers to individuals who did not have them. The area numbers of these dummy SSNs range from 900 through 999 and appeared on some military orders and unit rosters in the late 1960s and early 1970s. These dummy numbers were later replaced with valid Social Security numbers.

Group numbers (middle two digits) range from 01 to 99 but are not assigned in consecutive order. For administrative reasons, group numbers issued first consist of the odd numbers from 01 through 09 and then even numbers from 10 through 98, within each area number allocated to a state. After all even numbers 10 through 98 of a particular area have been issued, the even numbers 02 through 08 are used, followed by odd numbers 11 through 99, as shown:

ODD	EVEN	EVEN	ODD
01, 03, 05, 07,09	10 to 98	02, 04, 06, 08	11 to 99

Within each group, the *serial numbers* (last four digits of the Social Security number) run consecutively from 0001 through 9999.

Social Security Administration Bulletin Board

The Social Security Administration has a bulletin board that provides a great deal of information concerning itself and Social Security numbers.

For example, if you wanted to determine the highest group number that has been issued or the date a SSN was issued, you can access this information through this bulletin board. The computer modem number is (410) 965–1133. There is no charge for this service.

Chapter 13

OTHER METHODS

This chapter provides numerous ways to locate anyone, whether civilian or military. It explains how government agencies, publications, and private organizations may provide assistance.

Churches

Churches can be of great assistance in many searches. Most priests, ministers and rabbis know the addresses of their current and former members. Most churches and synagogues maintain records of membership, baptisms, confirmations, first communions, bar mitzvahs, weddings and burials. Also, many religious groups have church sponsored clubs and organizations which should be contacted for information. You should also contact other members of the church that the subject attended. If you know the religious affiliation of the person, this can be a place to obtain addresses and information (e.g., date of birth, former address, information concerning divorces, names and addresses of friends, relatives and former spouses).

Colleges, Universities and Alumni Associations

The federal Family and Educational Rights and Privacy Act allows colleges and universities to release "directory information" to the public without the consent of the student. A student may request that all or part of this information be withheld from the public by making a written request to do so (but few do). "Directory information" includes, but is not limited to, student's name, current address, telephone listing, major, date and place of birth, dates of attendance, degrees and awards received and previous educational agencies or institutions attended. Some colleges may release a student's SSN. Contact college registrars for this information.

College alumni associations try to keep current addresses of former students and most will either provide the address or will forward a letter. They also publish directories of former students (some list graduates only) with current addresses and employment. If the alumni association will not give you an address, then contact the college library, which will have a copy of the directory. They normally will provide you with an address or other identifying information. Alumni associations and college libraries will also have copies of yearbooks which can sometimes provide the individual's legal name, hometown, degree and other information. See *Peterson's Guide to Four-year Colleges* or *Accredited Institutions of Post Secondary Education* for additional information on this subject in the library section of this chapter.

Internet users see the World Alumni Homepage at http://www.infophil.com/world/alumni. They link to colleges and high schools around the world.

Congressional Assistance

If you are not getting results or answers from federal agencies or the military, you can write or call your United States Representative or Senator and ask for their assistance. Federal agencies and the armed forces are very responsive to inquiries from Members of Congress. You can expect a quick reply to your letter, usually within two weeks.

Include all the information you can about the person you are trying to locate, why you need to contact him, what steps you have taken so far and the results of these steps.

The telephone number for the U.S. Capitol in Washington, DC is (202) 224-3121. Tell the operator the name of your Senator or Representative and the state he represents. You will be connected to his office. To write your Representative, the address is:

Honorable (John Doe)
United States House of Representatives
Washington, DC 20515

To write your Senator the address is:

Honorable (John Doe)
United States Senate
Washington, DC 20510

See your local telephone book for your Congressman's name and telephone number. It will help if you call the local office first and talk to the administrative assistant about the difficulties you are encountering.

The Court House and City Hall

Government records such as deeds to property, automobile registration, marriage licenses, business names, voter registration, professional licenses, tax records, record of trials (civil or criminal) can be a source of information that can give you current addresses and possibly a SSN of people you are searching for. Military people often buy real estate near the bases where they are stationed. As they move, they usually rent out the property and the tax bill is mailed to them. This information is public record. Check both the courthouse and city hall for tax and deed information. This is best achieved by mail, in person or through computerized search services. In many areas utility users (water, gas, electricity, cable television) addresses are available, if requested.

Most employees in local government offices can be very helpful, especially if you tell them the urgency and reason for your search.

A trip to your local library can help you identify county and civil jurisdictions as well as their addresses. This information is also available in the *National ZIP Code Directory* published by the U.S. Postal Service.

Federal Parent Locator Service

The Federal government will make a computer search of IRS, VA, and Social Security files of anyone who has a child support order against them. You must provide the name and Social Security number of the person you are looking for.

To obtain a search, first contact the State Parent Locator Service in the Child Support Enforcement

Bureau of the state in which you reside. Check your local telephone directory for address and telephone number.

Immigration and Naturalization Service

The Immigration and Naturalization Service (INS) has duplicate records of all naturalizations that occurred after September 26, 1906. Inquiries about citizenship granted after that date should be sent to the INS on a form that can be obtained from any of the INS district offices. Local postmasters can provide the address of the nearest district office or check your telephone book. For additional information, write to:

Immigration and Naturalization Service
U.S. Department of Justice
425 "I" Street, N.W.
Washington, DC 20536
(202) 633-5231, (202) 633-3296 Fax

Internal Revenue Service

The Internal Revenue Service (IRS) will forward letters for humane reasons to people that they can identify with a Social Security number. Humane reasons are:

- Urgent or compelling nature, such as a serious illness.
- Imminent death or death of a close relative.
- A person seeking a missing relative.

A reunion or tracing a family tree does not qualify as a humane purpose. The IRS will not forward letters concerning debts. If a letter is forwarded by the IRS and is undeliverable by the post office and returned to the IRS, it will be destroyed and the sender will not be notified.

If an address can be found, the letter will be placed in an IRS envelope and the addressee will be advised that the letter is being forwarded in accordance with current IRS policy. The IRS will not divulge the recipient's current address, nor any tax information, and the decision to reply is entirely up to the recipient. Check your telephone book for the IRS office closest to you.

Obtain an Ex-Spouse's Social Security Number

An individual who is divorced and cannot remember the SSN of their former spouse may request a copy of any past joint income tax returns from the IRS for a small fee. These returns will contain the SSN of the former spouse.

Public Libraries

City and county public libraries have a wealth of information for searchers. The same may be true of college, private and other specialized libraries. These resources can be utilized either in person, by written communication, by telephone or fax. Visit your local library and ask the librarian for assistance. Tell the librarian what you are doing and you will definitely get a lot of valuable assistance. This is especially true for information in libraries located in cities where your subject once resided.

Many libraries take part in the Interlibrary Loan and the On-Line Computer Library Center Programs. With the Interlibrary Loan Program, one library might be able to send the books or materials you need to a library closer to you. With the On-Line Computer Library Center Program you can find out which libraries have what reference materials so you can go to that particular library. Ask your librarian for details and procedures.

Most military installations have base libraries and museums that probably have some information about the units that were stationed there. Call the information operator of the base concerned (see Base/Post Loators in Chapter Two) to obtain the telephone number of the base library and museum. Remember to ask for help from the library staff. See Chapter Eight for addresses of military base libraries.

Latter-day Saints Libraries

The Church of Jesus Christ of Latter-day Saints (Mormons) has the largest family history (genealogical) library in the world. They also operate numerous local family history libraries in major cities throughout the United States. These local libraries can obtain endless amounts of genealogical information from the main library in Salt Lake City and are extremely helpful to searchers. Many libraries have the Social Security Master Death Index, local birth and death records and excellent collections of local telephone books. For additional information, contact the nearest local family history library or write to:

Church of Jesus Christ of Latter-day Saints
Family History Department
35 North West Temple
Salt Lake City, UT 84150

Regional Government Depository Libraries

Many libraries are members of the Regional Government Depository Library Program. Although many public libraries and university libraries participate in this program, not all have the facilities for maintaining extensive collections of federal publications. Regional depositories are charged with receiving all new and revised government publications authorized for distribution to depository libraries.

Many documents and books published by the federal government and the armed forces can be borrowed by libraries who participate in this program from Regional Government Depository Libraries. These depository libraries are located in every state. Examples of publications that may be borrowed are armed forces officers registers, Department of State employee registers and lists, federal government telephone books, U.S. Government pamphlets on such diverse matters as census data, commercial laws, bankruptcy courts, federal tax matters, etc. Consider using this valuable resource if you are involved with a difficult search. Ask your librarian how you can use this service to obtain publications you may need.

You can use the services of these Regional Government Depositories directly. Call the Federal Information Center at (800) 688-9889 for the address and telephone number of the library closest to you.

Books and Other Resources

The following books and resources have proven to be valuable to searchers. We have divided them into the categories of General Reference, Search Related, and Databases and Microfilm Information.

—General Reference—

All in One Directory by Gebby Press. Contains addresses, telephone numbers and fax numbers of daily and weekly newspapers, radio and television stations, business, trade, black and Hispanic press, and general and consumer magazines. This unique publication is used by public relation firms and professional searchers.

Directories in Print. Lists the names and addresses of where to acquire membership directories of hundreds of trade organizations and professional associations.

Directory of American Libraries with Genealogical and Local History. Provides a comprehensive listing of private and public libraries in the U.S. which have genealogical and local history sections. Published by Ancestry.

Directory of Associations. Contains the addresses and telephone numbers of thousands of associations in the United States. The associations vary from business orientated, veterans groups, professional, trade and numerous other types. This information may be obtained on the internet at www.newmarket-forum.com/assoc.html

Directory of Special Libraries and Information Centers. Lists over 15,000 public libraries and over 19,000 special libraries, archives, research libraries and information centers in the United States.

Directory of United States Libraries. Lists all of the libraries in the country. Published by the American Library Association.

Knowing Where to Look: The Ultimate Guide to Research. Contains numerous ideas on using libraries.

Written by Lois Horowitz. Available from Writer's Digest Books.

The National Yellow Book of Funeral Directors. Lists names, addresses and telephone numbers of most funeral homes and directors in the United States. Listings are by city within each state. This is a priceless source of information for searchers who are attempting to locate information about a deceased person. Funeral directors keep files which may list names and addresses of relatives and friends of the deceased. This is a particularly valuable source if an obituary was not published or a death certificate is not obtainable.

National ZIP Code Directory. In addition to zip codes for every city and town in the nation, this book also identifies county and civil jurisdictions as well as their addresses. Published by the U.S. Postal Service, this book is also available for use or sale at all post offices.

Newspapers in Microform: United States. A helpful print reference for locating newspapers stored on microfilm. Published by the Library of Congress.

Order of Battle (1939–1946 U.S. Army). Lists all major and subordinate Army units involved in WWII. Written by Shelby L. Stanton.

Peterson's Guide to Four-year Colleges and *Accredited Institutions of Post Secondary Education.* Useful if you wish to obtain the address of an alumni association or a college library. If either group does not have a record of your subject, you may place a "locator notice" in the alumni publication.

U.S. Military Museums, Historic Sites and Exhibits, by Bruce D. Thompson and published by Military

Living, is one of the most comprehensive books available on this subject. It includes listings of Air Force, Army, Coast Guard, Marine Corps, Navy and NOAA museums in the United States and overseas. It also lists all American military cemeteries and military sites in the National Park System. This 300 page book is a must for people doing military research, reunion planning or who have an interest in our country's military history.

U.S. War Ships of WWII. A complete list of Army, Navy and Coast Guard ships used during WWII. Includes dates of commissioning and de-commissioning, and disposition of each de-commissioned ship. Written by Paul H. Silverstone. Published by the Naval Institute Press.

U.S. War Ships Since 1945. A complete list of Army, Navy and Coast Guard ships used since 1945. Includes dates of commissioning and de-commissioning, and disposition of each de-commissioned ship. Written by Paul H. Silverstone. Published by the Naval Institute Press.

Vietnam Order of Battle: Army and Allied Ground Forces and Air Force Units (1961–1973). Lists all major and subordinate Army and Air Force units involved in the Vietnam war. Written by Shelby L. Stanton.

Maps and atlases. Often a map is a valuable tool in a search to determine the location of a street or even the location of a city. Libraries have abundant maps that may be useful in your search.

—Search Related—

City Directories and *Crisscross Directories.* Public libraries, especially larger systems, maintain collections of city directories and criss-cross directories of their city and surrounding cities. These two directories can be some of your best search tools. Begin with the edition for the last year you knew your subject lived in a particular city. Check more current editions to find the last year he is listed and at which address. You can then identify neighbors or former neighbors who might know where the person now lives. You can also do a computer address update if the address is not over ten years old (see Appendix B). Call or write the library and ask them to search for you. In the event they will not search, ask them for names of local researchers you can contact. Also check with "People Searching News" (see page 234).

Telephone books. Many libraries maintain collections of old telephone books for their city and surrounding area. These telephone books can provide old addresses of your subject and often names and former addresses of spouses, children and other relatives. They are also sources of names of former employers (individual and business names). Use these books in conjunction with city directories.

Biographic Register. Annual list (register) of civil service employees published by the Department of State. It includes biographic information on State Department employees as well as personnel of the Agency for International Development, the Peace Corps, the Foreign Agricultural Service, and the United States Information Agency. Many registers include date and place of birth, colleges attended, foreign service posts, and spouse's name.

Birthright: The Guide to Search and Reunion for Adoptees, Birthparents and Adoptive Parents. Excellent resource for anyone trying to find a birth parent, adoptive parent or a child who was adopted. Written by Jean A. S. Strauss. Published by Penguin Books.

Dictionary of Surnames. In the event you are not sure of the spelling of a surname, this book by Patrick Hanks and Flavia Hodges has alternate spellings of thousands of surnames. It also explains the origin and meaning of over 70,000 surnames.

Find Anyone Fast by Phone, Fax, Mail and Computer. Essential resource on locating missing people. Hundreds of search techniques are explained as well as how to organize and conduct a search. Also includes computer searches that are available to the public. Written by Richard S. Johnson. Published by MIE Publishing.

Foreign Service Lists. Directories of Foreign Service officers that are published three times a year by the Department of State. These list field staffs of the U.S. Foreign Service, the U.S. Information Agency, AID, the Peace Corps, and the Foreign Agricultural Service. A brief job title appears, as well as date arrived in the country they are assigned and their civil service grade.

Military Officers Registers. Excellent resource for obtaining information on individuals who served as officers and warrant officers in the armed forces. Each branch of the service published a register of regular, reserved and retired officers annually. Earlier editions contain name, rank, service number, DOB, colleges and universities attended and some assignment information. Later editions (1968–80) list name, rank, SSN, DOB and other miscellaneous service data. Registers were discontinued in 1981 due to the Privacy Act. Some copies are available on microfiche.

U.S. Air Force Register. Annual list of commissioned officers—active and retired. Includes service number (pre mid-1969) or Social Security number and date of birth.

U.S. Army Register. Yearly lists of active, reserve and retired officers. Lists service number (pre mid-1969) or Social Security Number and date of birth. Pre-1969 active lists include state of birth and military training.

Register of Commissioned and Warrant Officers—Navy and Marine Corps and Reserve Officers on Active Duty—of the United States Naval Reserve; Register of Retired Commissioned and Warrant Officers, Regular and Reserve of the United States Navy and Marine Corps. Annual lists that include service number (pre-1972) or Social Security number and date of birth.

Directories of Alumni of the military academies: The *Register of Graduates of the United States Air Force Academy* has begun to appear in a "condensed" version. The 1989 register is the most recent "complete" version. It contains date of birth, full biographical sketches listing awards, decorations and special honors. Spouse's name and notations indicating most recently known place of employment may appear. Rank, reserve status, year and circumstance of leaving service also may appear. Names of deceased alumni appear in italics. Since 1994 this Register contains complete historical biographic information.

The *Register of Graduates and Former Cadets of the United States Military Academy* includes state and date of birth. Every effort has been made to include awards, separation dates and ranks, prior military service, colleges and degrees earned, current address and current employment. Deceased graduate's names are printed in italics.

The *Register of Alumni: Graduates and Former Naval Cadets and Midshipmen* includes date and place of birth, last known address, decorations and awards, special assignments, retirements and rank attained. Marine Corps officers are designated. A letter "D" denotes deceased alumni. If known, the name and address of the widow is included.

The MVR Book: Motor Services Guide. Describes in detail where and how to obtain driver and vehicle registration records in all states. This is one of the outstanding and easy to use public records research books, published by BRB Publications. Check this book before attempting to locate people through state drivers license and MVR offices.

Registers of doctors: *The Directory of Medical Specialists* by Marquis Who's Who, and *The American Medical Directory* published by the American Medical Association. Medical associations are excellent resources for locating doctors. Also state and county medical associations often publish registers and directories of their members. In addition to names, these books also provide information on medical specialty, schooling, business address, and other useful information.

The Sourcebook of Federal Courts: U.S. District and Bankruptcy. Provides complete information on how to obtain criminal and civil court records and bankruptcy files from federal courts. It outlines jurisdictions and boundaries of these courts. Federal court records may provide addresses of your subject as well as other individuals who may have knowledge of his former or present locations. Another excellent source book for searchers, published by BRB Publications.

The Sourcebook of State Public Records. Explains how to obtain records at the state level for business records, liens and security interest records, criminal records, workers compensation, vital records, MVR, occupational licensing, and business names and permits. Another essential reference book, published by BRB Publications.

Who's Who in America series. This series of books contains thousands of names and additional information on prominent people in many different career fields.

—Database and Microfilm Information—

The following have proven to be of immense value to searchers. There are numerous other resources available in libraries that can be of assistance also.

Computer Files and Searches. The National Telephone Directory and the Social Security Master Death Index are on CD-ROM at some larger libraries. It is also available through on-line services and the Internet. The National Telephone Directory contains over 90 million listings of people who have listed telephone numbers. The Social Security Master Death Index lists over 60 million people who have died since 1962.

Draft Registration Records. Some libraries have copies of draft registration records of their local county for World War I, II, Korean and Vietnam. These records contain legal names, addresses and DOBs.

Voter Registration Records. Libraries may have access to many years of voter registration lists from the board of elections (voter registration offices) of their local area. Most of these records contain legal names, addresses, DOB and SSN of registered voters.

Microfilm Files of Real Estate Owners. Lists (current and old) of real estate owners are often available in local libraries. This data is usually indexed by name and address.

Newsbank. Most libraries have access to local newspaper indexes that may list the name of the person you are seeking. In addition to news articles, names may be listed under birth, engagements, marriages, divorces, funeral, and death announcements. Many libraries can search national databases available through vendors. Searches can be made for an individual whose name appears in a major newspaper or who may be an officer of a company (even a sole proprietorship). Check with your librarian concerning capabilities for searches and fees.

Newspaper Obituary Files. Most libraries maintain an obituary file of local deaths. This information is usually obtained from local newspapers and goes back many years. Most libraries will respond to telephone request for information from these files. Others will only respond to a written request and some require a search fee. Their response time is usually a few days and some libraries will fax you the requested information. The information section is usually the place where the obituary file is kept; however, some libraries keep it in their genealogical section.

Phonefiche. Many main libraries have telephone directories of many cities in the nation on microfiche. In the event the library does not have the National Telephone Directory on CD-ROM, Phonefiche is a good alternative source of addresses and telephone numbers. The disadvantage is that you must look through each city for listings and addresses. You cannot do a national search with this system as you can with the CD-ROM version of the telephone files.

Locating Military Dependents

Sometimes the best way to contact or locate an individual is by first locating their children. The following organizations may be of help.

—Military Brats of America—

Military Brats of America (MBA) is an organization for all current and former armed forces dependents, foreign service dependents, and spouses of either. Members network together, provide detailed background information about duty tours and schools, publish a magazine called *Brats*, plan events and participate in charitable activities. MBA is also compiling a comprehensive roster of all Military Brats from 1901 through the present. The roster will become accessible by telephone in 1997.

MBA also sponsors the MBA electronic bulletin boards on America On-Line and CompuServe which are accessed by several hundred thousand military brats. These bulletin boards list reunion information, a locator service for individuals, and dozens of topics of interest.

Military Brats of America   (212) 689-5208
PO Box 1165
New York, NY 10159-1165
(military,command post) bratnews@aol.com
Compuserve (Go Brats) 76711.675

—Overseas Brats—

Overseas Brats is an umbrella organization for over 200 alumni associations of overseas American private, State Department, and Department of Defense high schools. The combined membership of former students and faculty members totals more than 60,000.

While Overseas Brats does not maintain a list of individual students, it does maintain a list of active alumni associations. Requests for specific alumni associations can be made to:

Overseas Brats
PO Box 29805
San Antonio, TX 78229
(210) 349-1394
http://www.vni.net/~mcl/osb/osbmain.htm

—American Overseas Schools Archives—

The American Overseas Schools Archives, under the supervision of the American Overseas Schools Historical Society (AOSHS), was established in 1989. It was organized to collect, record and preserve histories and memorabilia of Department of Defense overseas schools which have served American students for 50 years. The archive has memorabilia pertaining to all aspects of overseas schools from kindergarten through high school. It includes hundreds of thousands of items such as yearbooks, scrapbooks, curricula, newspaper, magazine and journal articles, photographs, official papers and documents, personal histories and memorabilia of all kinds. AOSHS publishes a quarterly newsletter. For more information, contact:

American Overseas Schools
  Historical Society
PO Box 777
Lichfield Park, AZ 83340
(602) 935-3939
hmyq24a@prodigy.com

Newspapers and Magazines

When seeking current or former military people, the following weekly newspapers are recommended: *Army Times, Navy Times, Navy Times: Marine Corps Edition, Air Force Times,* and *Federal Times.* These are the most popular and most widely read newspapers of Armed Services and Civil Service personnel. *Federal Times* is read primarily by present and former Civil Servants, a large portion of whom are military veterans, retired military or members of the Reserve Components. These newspapers have locator columns that may help. Readers include current military members, but also many reserve, National Guard, retired and veterans. You will probably get a response to any published notice. Following is the address for all the above newspapers:

Army Times Publishing Company
6883 Commercial Drive
Springfield, VA 22159
(800) 424-9335

The largest veteran oriented newspaper in the United States is *Stars and Stripes: The National Tribune.* When seeking a veteran or publicizing a reunion, this publication should be considered.

Stars and Stripes: The National Tribune
PO Box 1803
Washington, DC 20013
(202) 829-3225, (202) 829-5657 Fax

The *Airborne Static Line* is a monthly publication for, by, and about paratroopers and men with airborne hearts. This publication is dedicated to the perpetuation of the airborne ideals of brotherhood, fellowship and camaraderie established in warfare, strife and duress of combat. Published 12 times per year, dues for this publication are $30 per year. The *Airborne Static Line* publishes a locator column in every edition.

Airborne Static Line
PO Box 87518
College Park, GA 30337
(770) 478-5301, (770) 961-2838 Fax

A particularly effective newspaper is the one sold in the last known location where the person you are seeking lived. Place an advertisement in the personal section. Thousands of people read the classified section and you may get a response. Write an advertisement similar to the following:

> **Chief Master Sgt. Joe L. James**
> Urgent, anyone who knows his
> whereabouts call collect (513) 555-5555.

Also, a letter to the editor of such a newspaper may bring you some help in your search. Check *Gale's Directory of Publications* in your local library for names and addresses of most newspapers in the U.S.

People Searching News (PSN) is an excellent magazine with emphasis on adoption and missing person searches ($18, six issues per year; a sample copy + registry forms are $6.95). *PSN* sells a variety of search books and can offer the services of more than 1,000 researchers world-wide. *PSN* also has a large "in-search-of" classified ad section; subscribers are likely to offer you help and information. Their no-fee search hot-line is (407) 768-2222.

People Searching News
PO Box 100444
Palm Bay, FL 32910-0444

Locating People in Prison

All states operate prison locators, usually through the State Department of Corrections. If the individual you are looking for is possibly in a federal prison, telephone the U.S. prison federal locator at (202) 307-3126. Aliases may be available. To determine if a former military member is or has been imprisoned in the U.S. Disciplinary Barracks (military prison) at Ft. Leavenworth, Kansas, call (913) 684-4629 or 684-4743. Most prison locators keep records of former inmates for up to ten years. Surname searches may be completed without date of birth or Social Security number.

Locating People Traveling Overseas

To locate U.S. citizens traveling abroad call the State Department's Citizens Emergency Center: (202) 647-5225.

Locating Pilots Who Are Licensed by the FAA

The Federal Aviation Administration (FAA) will provide a pilot's current address if you provide the name and date of birth, or a SSN or certificate number. If the name is unique, they can provide the information without these identifying items. The pilot's records are annotated with the name and address of the person who requested the information.

FAA Airmen Certification Branch, AVN-460
PO Box 25082
Oklahoma City, OK 73125
(405) 954-3261

Locating Civil Service Employees

Thousands of veterans and retired military are employed by the federal Civil Service because of military experience and hiring preference.

The Office of Personnel Management operates a centralized service that will locate most federal civil service employees. However, they will not locate employees of the judicial and congressional offices, U.S. Postal Service, TVA, General Accounting Office, FBI, DEA and other intelligence agencies.

The only information that is permitted to be released is the name and address of the individual's employing agency, the location of his actual place of employment or the address of the agency's personnel office. The latter will provide address of work site if their policy permits.

To request a search, submit the person's name and Social Security number. Allow two weeks for replies to written requests. Telephone requests will only be taken for one or two names.

U.S. Office of Personnel Management
1900 "E" Street, N.W., Room 7494
Washington, DC 20415

The U.S. Postal Service

For many years you could obtain an individual's new address from the U.S. Post Office under the FOIA if the individual had submitted a change-of-address card. This practice was discontinued as of April 1994. However, the U.S. Postal Change-of-Address file is still available to credit bureaus, other information providers, and in many computer databases (see Appendix B).

You may still be able to obtain an individual's new address by doing the following: mail a letter to the person you are seeking to the last known address and write "ADDRESS CORRECTION REQUESTED" on the lower edge of the envelope or below the return address. The post office will place a label showing the new address and return your letter to you. You may also put "DO NOT FORWARD" and the letter will be returned to you with the individual's new address. Change of address information is retained by the post office for eighteen months, but they will forward mail for only 12 months. There is a fee of thirty five cents for this service. You might want to use this method when you forward letters through the armed forces World-Wide Locators, base locators, alumni associations and the Social Security Administration. You may find the person's current address in this manner.

You may also write the postmaster (especially smaller towns) of the town where the person once lived. You might obtain some useful information and assistance. Many small town postmasters have held their job for 30 to 40 years and know the location or relatives of numerous people who once lived there.

Using Professional Searchers

Some difficult cases may need the help of a professional searcher. These can include private investigators, specialized searchers and attorneys. Listed below are professionals recommended by the author.

The National Association of Investigative Specialists (NAIS) is a world-wide network of private investigative professionals and/or agencies. With over 1,500 members, it is one of the largest associations in the world for private investigators.

National Association of Investigative Specialists
PO Box 33244
Austin, TX 78764
(512) 928-8190

Darrin Fansler is a private investigator who resides and practices in Germany. He is a former U.S. Army Military Police investigator. He specializes in locating active and retired U.S. military who are stationed or reside in Germany. He is also available for debt collection, background investigation, etc. For information and fees, contact:

Detective Darrin Fansler
PO Box 27392
Tampa, FL 33685
(813) 963-0499 Information
011-49-6188-5280 (office in Germany)

Charles Eric Gordon is an attorney concentrating on locating persons who have been missing for a substantial period of time or about whom little information is known. He is a consultant to law firms, corporations, government agencies and foreign governments in tracing missing witnesses, heirs, beneficiaries, relatives, debtors and others.

With his world-wide contacts and many years of experience as both an attorney and an investigator, he can also assist in obtaining information and public records which are difficult to access, e.g., vital records, voter registration and court records.

Charles Eric Gordon, Esq.
5 Joyce Road
PO Box 514
Plainview, NY 11803-0514
(516) 433-5065

Locating American Fathers of Amerasians

Samantha Wright conducts searches for U.S. military fathers of Asian American children. She has extensive information on military personnel (all branches) who served in the Vietnam era. She maintains a registry of thousands of children born in Vietnam who are searching for their American fathers. Searches can be provided for fathers looking for their Amerasian children. Information and fees, contact:

Samantha Wright
Asian American Initiatives
343 Marvin Avenue
Brooks, KY 40109-5229
(502) 955-8047, phone/fax

Locating American Fathers of European Children

Lt. Col. Philip C. Grinton (Ret) assists the children of British mothers to find their American GI fathers. His main area of expertise is finding men who served in the European Theater of Operation during World War II. For information and fees, contact:

Lt. Col. Philip C. Grinton (Ret)
828 Beaver Street
Santa Rosa, CA 95404-3731
(707) 545-1520, E-mail: philgrin@aol.com

Locating People in German Speaking Countries

The following team of searchers specialize in locating people (birth parents, children and others) who live or have lived in Germany, Austria or Switzerland. Both were born in Germany and have extensive experience and numerous contacts in Europe. For information and fees, contact:

Leonie Boehmer	Margit S. Benton
805 Alvarado, N.E.	38 Bailey Drive
Albuquerque, NM 87108	Charleston, SC 29405
(505) 268-1310	(803) 747-6156

The Salvation Army

The Salvation Army conducts searches of missing people for immediate family members only, through their national missing person network. Contact your local Salvation Army Social Service Center for information and a registration form. There is a $10 fee for this service.

There are also four territorial headquarters for the Salvation Army that can assist you in a search. Regional addresses for the Salvation Army Missing Persons Services are:

Southern U.S. Salvation Army
Missing Persons Services
1424 N.E. Expressway
Atlanta, GA 30329

Western U.S. Salvation Army
Missing Persons Service
30840 Hawthorne Boulevard
Rancho Palos Verdes, CA 90274

Eastern U.S. Missing Persons Services
120 W. 14th Street
New York, NY 10011

Central U.S. Salvation Army
Missing Persons Services
860 N. Dearborn Street
Chicago, IL 60610

Social Security Administration

The Social Security Administration (SSA) will forward some unsealed letters to people whose names are listed in their files. This will be done for certain humanitarian reasons that will be beneficial to the receiver, e.g., locating missing relatives, medical needs, locating heirs to estates, assisting people with claims, etc. Letters that are accepted will be forwarded to their employers or directly to the individual if he is drawing Social Security benefits.

Before offering assistance, the SSA must determine that the person to be contacted would want to receive the letter and would want to reply.

The SSA will not forward any correspondence unless strong compelling reasons exist. For example:

- A strong humanitarian purpose will be served (e.g., a close relative is seriously ill, is dying or has died).
- A minor is left without parental guidance.
- A defendant in a felony case is seeking a defense witness.
- A parent wishes to locate a son or daughter. Consent of the missing person is needed in connection with an adoption proceeding for his/her child.
- The missing person would want to know the contents of the letter.
- The missing person's disappearance occurred recently enough that SSA could reasonably expect to have a usable mailing address.
- All other possibilities for contacting the missing person have been exhausted.

You must submit your request in writing to the SSA, giving the following information:

- Missing person's name and Social Security number (SSN).
- If SSN is unknown, give date and place of birth, name of parents, name and address of last known employer and period of employment.

- Reason for wanting to contact the person.
- Last time seen.
- Other contacts that have been exhausted.

Enclose your letter to be forwarded in an unsealed stamped envelope. SSA will try to find an address in their records for the missing person. If an address is found they will forward your letter. They will tell you if they cannot forward a letter because they cannot locate a Social Security number for the missing person. They cannot tell you whether:

- They found an address for the missing person.
- They were able to forward a letter to the missing person.

A strong compelling reason may be deemed to exist if a monetary or other consideration is involved and it is reasonable to assume that the missing person does not know it. For example:

- Missing person is a beneficiary of an estate.
- Insurance proceeds are due the person.
- An important document is being held. (SSA will not forward the document.)

The procedures are the same as above except include a personal check, cashier's check, or money order payable to the Social Security Administration in the amount of $3 per letter.

Always ask for a receipt if you make a payment as sometimes the clerks will write the individual's SSN on the receipt. Also, if you are seeking someone who has changed their name, the new name may be listed on the receipt. If you do obtain a receipt with some new information on it, you can then attempt some of the computer searches listed in Appendix B.

In the event they cannot help you and you have prepaid a fee, the Treasury Department will send you a refund. They will state that you overpaid them or that they do not charge a fee in your case. Mail all correspondence to:

Social Security Administration
Office of Central Records Operations
300 N. Greene Street
Baltimore, MD 21201
(800) 772-1213

Telephone Company

Contact your local telephone company and ask if they have telephone books for other cities, especially if the local library does not have the ones you need.

The directory assistance operator (long distance information) can give you valuable information in addition to telephone numbers. You can request Directory Assistance to check the entire area code for the person you are seeking. Most area code operators will do this search for you. Dial 1-XXX-555-1212 where XXX is the area code you are seeking.

You can get addresses or you can find out if a certain person has a telephone even if it is unlisted in some areas. There are different rules in each state and area code concerning unlisted telephone numbers. If you find out the person does have an unlisted number, call the operator and have them call and ask them to contact you. This service is done only in some areas for emergencies or important matters. Many people can be located easily through the telephone company or using telephone books.

About the Author

Lt. Col. Richard (Dick) S. Johnson (Ret) served 28 years in the U.S. Army in various positions involving personnel records and management, military postal operations and automated data processing. The latter involved the collection of military personnel records on computers and the operation of two Army locators. He served tours in Germany, Italy, Korea and Vietnam and was stationed at numerous bases in the United States. He retired in 1979. He received several Army decorations for outstanding and meritorious service including the Bronze Star Medal, four awards of the Meritorious Service Medal and The Army Commendation Medal.

For the last several years he has done extensive research on methods of locating current and former members of the military. In 1988 he wrote the first edition of *How to Locate Anyone Who Is or Has Been in the Military* and since has written *Find Anyone Fast*, and *Secrets of Finding Unclaimed Money*. Dick writes a column entitled "Searching" that is published monthly in *Stars and Stripes* newspaper, *Military*, and *Reunions* magazine.

Dick has appeared on numerous TV and radio shows, has been the subject of several newspaper and magazine articles and is a frequent speaker on the subject of locating missing people. Dick has located people for TV shows, reunion organizations, attorneys, private investigators, heir searchers, people seeking missing relatives and birth parents and many other individuals. He assisted the 11th Armored Cavalry's Veterans of Vietnam and Cambodia in locating over 18,000 of their former members.

Dick lives in San Antonio, Texas with his wife Mickey and their dog Ashley.

FORMS AND WORKSHEETS

Individual Data Worksheet

PERSONAL INFORMATION

Complete name, nicknames, maiden name, previous married
names, and aliases _____

_____

Social Security number (SSN)

Date of birth _____

Place of birth_____

Driver/motorcycle license (list state) _____

Physical description: height, weight, color of hair and eyes,
tattoos, scars, etc. (obtain photos) _____

_____

EDUCATION

Schools attended: elementary, high school, college/universities,
dates attended _____

_____

Degrees earned _____

Professional memberships/licenses_____

_____

EMPLOYMENT

Dates and places of employment _____

_____

_____

Union membership _____

_____

FINANCIAL

Real Estate owned_____

Automobiles, motorcycles, boats owned (state of registration)

_____

Dates and places of bankruptcy _____

MILITARY SERVICE

Branch of military _____

Service number _____

Dates of service_____

Unit or ship assigned _____

Installation or base assigned_____

Wartime service _____

Rank or rating (if not known, officer or enlisted) _____

VA claim number/VA insurance number _____

Membership in veterans and military reunion organizations

_____

Membership in the reserve or National Guard; units/dates of
  assignment _____

MISCELLANEOUS

Church or synagogue affiliation _____

Lodges, fraternal and service organization membership

_____

Licenses: hunting, fishing, boating, amateur radio, pilot, etc.

_____

Hobbies, talents and avocations _____

Political party affiliation_____

Voter registration (list state) _____

Foreign and national travel history_____

Names, addresses and telephone numbers of friends and fellow
  employees_____

_____

Miscellaneous information _____

_____

Obtaining Military Records

The U.S. Locator Service (not affiliated with the Federal Government) can acquire records rapidly from the National Personnel Records Center and the Army Reserve Personnel Center in St. Louis, MO. All requests are properly prepared and hand-carried to the appropriate Center, thus assuring that you will receive the records you need in the most rapid manner possible. The following records may be obtained:

- Certified copies of *Report of Separation (DD 214)* for anyone discharged or retired from any of the armed forces, and army reservists who have been separated from active duty. Fee is $50. Allow four to six weeks for delivery.

- A copy of the *complete military personnel and medical records* (every item in the file is copied) of an individual can be provided to the veteran or his next of kin, if the veteran is deceased. Fee is $100. This includes records of individuals who are retired from any armed forces, most individuals who are discharged and have no reserve obligation (all branches), and current members of the Army reserve. Copies of military records of individuals on active duty, current members of the Army National Guard and Air National Guard, current members of the Navy, Marine and Air Force reserves cannot be obtained. These records are not at St. Louis, MO.*

Note: Requests for DD 214 and military records are made with the authorization form shown on the next page. It must be completed and signed by the veteran or his next of kin, if deceased. Please include proof of death (e.g., death certificate, obituary or funeral card).

- Certified copies of **complete military personnel and medical records** may also be obtained for attorneys and private investigators in four to six weeks for court cases. A court order signed by a federal or state judge is required. A sample of how the court order should be worded will be mailed or faxed upon request. The fee for this service is $200.*

- **Organizational records** can also be obtained. Write for details.

All fees are for research and in the event the records requested are not available or have been destroyed, the fee is not refundable. All requests must be prepaid and all information concerning the request should be included. All orders are shipped by first class mail but may be shipped by Federal Express for an additional fee of $10. Checks should be made payable to U.S. Locator Service (not affiliated with the federal government) or you may make payment by credit card. For additional information or to order records, mail or fax authorization to:

U.S. Locator Service
PO Box 2577
St. Louis, MO 63114-2577
(314) 423-0860

* Some records were destroyed in a fire in 1973 at the NPRC. See page 153 for additional information.

Military Records Authorization

I request and authorize that representatives of U.S. Locator Service be allowed to review my Military and/or Civilian Service Personnel and Medical Records, and/or Auxiliary Records in the same manner as if I presented myself for this purpose. I specifically authorize the National Personnel Records Center, St. Louis, MO, or other custodians of my military records, to release to U.S. Locator Service a complete copy of my military personnel and related medical records.

I am willing that a photocopy and or Fax of this authorization be considered as effective and valid as the original.

Signature _____ Date _____

If veteran is deceased, date of death and relationship

_____

(Please type or print.)

Name _____

| Last | First | Middle initial |

_____

Street address   Apt. #

_____

City   State   Zip Code

Social Security No. _____ Phone No. _____

Date of birth_____Place of birth _____

Service number _____Branch of service _____

Dates of service _____Rank _____

Current military status ( ) reserve, ( ) retired,
( ) separated with Army reserve obligation, ( ) none

Please obtain: ( ) DD 214, ( ) complete military records,
( ) other _____

Enclosed is ( ) check, ( ) money order; charge my ( ) Visa
( ) MasterCard   ( ) AMEX for $ _____

Card number _____ Exp. date _____

Signature _____

Address of where records are to be sent, if different from above:

_____

REQUEST PERTAINING TO MILITARY RECORDS

Please read instructions on the reverse. If more space is needed, use plain paper.

SECTION I—INFORMATION NEEDED TO LOCATE RECORDS *(Furnish as much as possible)*

1. NAME USED DURING SERVICE *(Last, first, and middle)*	2. SOCIAL SECURITY NO.	3. DATE OF BIRTH	4. PLACE OF BIRTH

5. ACTIVE SERVICE, PAST AND PRESENT *(For an effective records search, it is important that ALL service be shown below)*

BRANCH OF SERVICE (Also, show last organization, if known)	DATES OF ACTIVE SERVICE		Check one		SERVICE NUMBER DURING THIS PERIOD
	DATE ENTERED	DATE RELEASED	OFFI-CER	EN-LISTED	

6. RESERVE SERVICE, PAST OR PRESENT *If "none," check here* ▶ ☐

a. BRANCH OF SERVICE	b. DATES OF MEMBERSHIP		c. Check one		d. SERVICE NUMBER DURING THIS PERIOD
	FROM	TO	OFFI-CER	EN-LISTED	
			☐	☐	

7. NATIONAL GUARD MEMBERSHIP *(Check one):* ☐ a. ARMY ☐ b. AIR FORCE ☐ c. NONE

d. STATE	e. ORGANIZATION	f. DATES OF MEMBERSHIP		g. Check one		h. SERVICE NUMBER DURING THIS PERIOD
		FROM	TO	OFFI-CER	EN-LISTED	
				☐	☐	

8. IS SERVICE PERSON DECEASED
☐ YES ☐ NO   *If "yes," enter date of death.*

9. IS (WAS) INDIVIDUAL A MILITARY RETIREE OR FLEET RESERVIST ☐ YES ☐ NO

SECTION II—REQUEST

1. EXPLAIN WHAT INFORMATION OR DOCUMENTS YOU NEED; OR, CHECK ITEM 2; OR, COMPLETE ITEM 3	2. IF YOU ONLY NEED A STATEMENT OF SERVICE check here ☐

3. LOST SEPARATION DOCUMENT REPLACEMENT REQUEST *(Complete a or b, and c.)*

☐ a. REPORT OF SEPARATION *(DD Form 214 or equivalent)*	YEAR ISSUED	This contains information normally needed to determine eligibility for benefits. It may be furnished only to the veteran, the surviving next of kin, or to a representative with veteran's signed release (Item 5 of this form)
☐ b. DISCHARGE CERTIFICATE	YEAR ISSUED	This shows only the date and character of discharge. It is of little value in determining eligibility for benefits. It may be issued only to veterans discharged honorably or under honorable conditions, or, if deceased, to the surviving spouse.

c. EXPLAIN HOW SEPARATION DOCUMENT WAS LOST

4. EXPLAIN PURPOSE FOR WHICH INFORMATION OR DOCUMENTS ARE NEEDED

6. REQUESTER

a. IDENTIFICATION *(check appropriate box)*
☐ Same person identified in Section I   ☐ Surviving spouse
☐ Next of kin (relationship) _____
☐ Other (specify)

b. SIGNATURE *(see instruction 3 on reverse side)*	DATE OF REQUEST

5. RELEASE AUTHORIZATION, IF REQUIRED *(Read instruction 3 on reverse side)*

I hereby authorize release of the requested information/documents to the person indicated at right (Item 7).

VETERAN SIGN HERE ▶ _____

(If signed by other than veteran show relationship to veteran.)

7. Please type or print clearly — COMPLETE RETURN ADDRESS

Name, number and street, city, State and ZIP code

TELEPHONE NO. *(include area code)* ▶

INSTRUCTIONS

1. **Information needed to locate records.** Certain identifying information is necessary to determine the location of an individual's record of military service. Please give careful consideration to and answer each item on this form. If you do not have and cannot obtain the information for an item, show "NA," meaning the information is "not available." Include as much of the requested information as you can. This will help us to give you the best possible service.

2. **Charges for service.** A nominal fee is charged for certain types of service. In most instances service fees cannot be determined in advance. If your request involves a service fee you will be notified as soon as that determination is made.

3. **Restrictions on release of information.** Information from records of military personnel is released subject to restrictions imposed by the military departments consistent with the provisions of the Freedom of Information Act of 1967 (as amended in 1974) and the Privacy Act of 1974. A service person has access to almost any information contained in his own record. The next of kin, if the veteran is deceased, and Federal officials for official purposes, are authorized to receive information from a military service or medical record only as specified in the above cited Acts. Other requesters must have the release authorization, in item 5 of the form, signed by the veteran or, if deceased, by the next of kin. Employers

and others needing proof of military service are expected to accept the information shown on documents issued by the Armed Forces at the time a service person is separated.

4. **Location of military personnel records.** The various categories of military personnel records are described in the chart below. For each category there is a code number which indicates the address at the bottom of the page to which this request should be sent. For each military service there is a note explaining approximately how long the records are held by the military service before they are transferred to the National Personnel Records Center, St. Louis. Please read these notes carefully and make sure you send your inquiry to the right address. Please note especially that the record is not sent to the National Personnel Records Center as long as the person retains any sort of reserve obligation, whether drilling or non-drilling.

(If the person has two or more periods of service within the same branch, send your request to the office having the record for the last period of service.)

5. **Definitions for abbreviations used below:**
NPRC — National Personnel Records Center   PERS — Personnel Records
TDRL — Temporary Disability Retirement List   MED — Medical Records

SERVICE	NOTE: (See paragraph 4 above.)	CATEGORY OF RECORDS — WHERE TO WRITE ADDRESS CODE	▼
AIR FORCE (USAF)	Except for TDRL and general officers retired with pay, Air Force records are transferred to NPRC from Code 1, 90 days after separation and from Code 2, 150 days after separation.	Active members (includes National Guard on active duty in the Air Force), TDRL, and general officers retired with pay.	1
		Reserve, retired reservist on nonpay status, current National Guard officers not on active duty in Air Force, and National Guard released from active duty in Air Force.	2
		Current National Guard enlisted not on active duty in Air Force.	13
		Discharged, deceased, and retired with pay.	14
COAST GUARD (USCG)	Coast Guard officer and enlisted records are transferred to NPRC 7 months after separation.	Active, reserve, and TDRL members.	3
		Discharged, deceased, and retired members (see next item).	14
		Officers separated before 1/1/29 and enlisted personnel separated before 1/1/15.	6
MARINE CORPS (USMC)	Marine Corps records are transferred to NPRC between 8 and 9 months after separation.	Active, TDRL, and Selected Marine Corps Reserve members.	4
		Individual Ready Reserve and Fleet Marine Corps Reserve members.	5
		Discharged, deceased, and retired members (see next item).	14
		Members separated before 1/1/1905.	6
ARMY (USA)	Army records are transferred to NPRC as follows: Active Army and Individual Ready Reserve Control Groups: About 60 days after separation. U.S. Army Reserve Troop Unit personnel: About 120 to 180 days after separation.	Reserve, living retired members, retired general officers, and active duty records of current National Guard members who performed service in the U.S. Army before 7/1/72.*	7
		Active officers (including National Guard on active duty in the U.S. Army).	8
		Active enlisted (including National Guard on active duty in the U.S. Army) and enlisted TDRL.	9
		Current National Guard officers not on active duty in the U.S. Army.	12
		Current National Guard enlisted not on active duty in the U.S. Army.	13
		Discharged and deceased members (see next item).	14
		Officers separated before 7/1/17 and enlisted separated before 11/1/12.	6
		Officers and warrant officers TDRL.	8
NAVY (USN)	Navy records are transferred to NPRC 6 months after retirement or complete separation.	Active members (including reservists on duty) — PERS and MED	10
		Discharged, deceased, retired (with and without pay) less than six months, TDRL, drilling and nondrilling reservists. PERS ONLY	10
		MED ONLY	11
		Discharged, deceased, retired (with and without pay) more than six months (see next item) — PERS & MED	14
		Officers separated before 1/1/03 and enlisted separated before 1/1/1886 — PERS and MED	6

*Code 12 applies to active duty records of current National Guard officers who performed service in the U.S. Army after 6/30/72.
Code 13 applies to active duty records of current National Guard enlisted members who performed service in the U.S. Army after 6/30/72.

ADDRESS LIST OF CUSTODIANS (BY CODE NUMBERS SHOWN ABOVE) — Where to write / send this form for each category of records

1	Air Force Manpower and Personnel Center Military Personnel Records Division Randolph AFB, TX 78150-6001	5	Marine Corps Reserve Support Center 10950 El Monte Overland Park, KS 66211-1408	8	USA MILPERCEN ATTN: DAPC-MSR 200 Stovall Street Alexandria, VA 22332-0400	12	Army National Guard Personnel Center Columbia Pike Office Building 5600 Columbia Pike Falls Church, VA 22041
2	Air Reserve Personnel Center Denver, CO 80280-5000	6	Military Archives Division National Archives and Records Administration Washington, DC 20408	9	Commander U.S. Army Enlisted Records and Evaluation Center Ft. Benjamin Harrison, IN 46249-5301	13	The Adjutant General (of the appropriate State, DC, or Puerto Rico)
3	Commandant U.S. Coast Guard Washington, DC 20593-0001	7	Commander U.S. Army Reserve Personnel Center ATTN: DARP-PAS 9700 Page Boulevard St. Louis, MO 63132-5200	10	Commander Naval Military Personnel Command ATTN: NMPC-036 Washington, DC 20370-5036	14	National Personnel Records Center (Military Personnel Records) 9700 Page Boulevard St. Louis, MO 63132
4	Commandant of the Marine Corps (Code MMRB-10) Headquarters, U.S. Marine Corps Washington, DC 20380-0001			11	Naval Reserve Personnel Center New Orleans, LA 70146-5000		

☆ USGPO 1987- 181-032/50709

STANDARD FORM 180 BACK (Rev. 1-86)

LOCATOR SERVICES

The Nationwide Locator is a professional locator service that performs computer searches to provide addresses and other important information to the public. They provide information to attorneys, private investigators, collection agencies, reunion planners and others seeking information about friends or relatives. Their data is obtained from highly accurate and reasonably priced databases that contain information on over 1 billion records.

Here are the types of searches the Nationwide Locator provides:

Social Security search

Provide a name and nine digit Social Security number (SSN) and receive the person's most current reported address, date reported, and all previous reported addresses (if the SSN is contained in a national credit file). If a report of death has been submitted, it will be listed. $30 per SSN for a nationwide search.

Retrace

Provide a name and previous address (not over 6 years old) and receive a current address and Social Security number. $30 per name submitted.

Address update

Provide a name and last known address (not over ten years old) and receive the most current reported address and the names and telephone numbers of five neighbors. $30 per name submitted.

National Surname search

Provide a first name, middle initial and last name and the National Telephone Directory will be used to provide the names, addresses and listed telephone numbers of everyone in the nation with a matching name. $30 per name submitted.

Date of Birth search

Provide first and last name, approximate date or year of birth and Social Security number (if known) and receive all matching names, city and state of residence. May be able to provide street address and phone number. $75 per name and date of birth submitted.

Social Security Death Index search

Provide either the name and date of birth, name and Social Security number, or name only and receive a list of people who are deceased, their SSN, date of birth, and the date and place of death as reported by the Social Security Administration. $30 per name.

Information will normally be provided to you within 24 hours of receipt. Information will be returned by mail or by fax, if requested. Volume discounts are available. Prices are subject to change without notice. Other specialized searches are available.

Texas residents add 7.75% tax to above fees.

Client agrees that all information obtained through the Nationwide Locator will be used for lawful purposes and agrees to hold the Nationwide Locator harmless for any use of this service. Client states that the client understands and agrees the Nationwide Locator does not warrant and does not guarantee information obtained from database searches. Client agrees to pay for all searches made by the Nationwide Locator regardless of results (to include "no record"). The Nationwide Locator is owned by Military Information Enterprises, Inc., is a member of the San Antonio Retail Merchants Association and is listed by Dun and Bradstreet.

If you would like the Nationwide Locator to perform any of these searches, please write or fax the information required to perform the search along with the following:

1. Payment in full: check, money order or credit card. If using Visa, MasterCard or American Express, please include your card number, the expiration date, the amount charged, and your signature.
2. Your name.
3. Your phone number.
4. Your address, including city, state and zip code.
5. A self-addressed stamped business size envelope.
7. Fax number, if information is returned by fax.

The Nationwide Locator
PO Box 39903
San Antonio, Texas 78218
(210) 828-4667 Fax

—Notes—

COMPUTER ACCESS PACKAGES

The Nationwide Locator markets two computer access packages to locate missing people. These packages are for use by private investigators, collection agencies, attorneys, reunion planners, and others who are searching for a large number of people.

The Nationwide Locator Direct Access Package is a low-cost program that lets you enter the finest database in the country through which you can obtain addresses of people at the lowest possible price. There are no restrictions to who can use Nationwide Locator Direct Access Package. The database does not provide any credit information or reports. None of the provided information is regulated by the Fair Credit Reporting Act. This access package includes five major categories of searches:

- Social Security trace
- Social Security number retrace (criss-cross)
- Subject verification
- Address verification
- Telephone number ownership

All searches are on-line and receive instant responses. Most searches are $6 each. Social Security traces are less with volume usage.

- No minimum usage requirements
- No monthly user fee

- No large up-front fee
- No line charge
- Instant reports
- 24-hour-a-day access
- User-friendly access program

An IBM compatible computer, a modem, a telephone and a major credit card (VISA, MasterCard or American Express) are the only requirements. The cost of this package is $290.

The **NIS On-Line Information Services** is the nation's most versatile computer access package, and provides access to the files of all major information databases. This package is used by hundreds of private investigators, researchers and other professionals. Some of the available searches are:

- Social Security searches
- National criss-cross
- Surname searches
- Address updates
- Name and date-of-birth searches
- Postal forwarding
- Asset searches
- Commercial credit
- Motor vehicle registration traces
- Driver license traces
- Criminal history
- Worker's compensation
- Numerous other on-line searches

The cost of each search varies. Most searches give instant on-line results, while some searches will be returned within 3–5 days. A computer is not a requirement to use this program. It can be accessed by phone, fax, mail or e-mail 24 hours a day. The cost of this program is $395.

For more information concerning the Nation-wide Locator Direct Access Package or NIS On-Line Information Services contact:

The Nationwide Locator
PO Box 39903
San Antonio, TX 78218
(210) 828-4667 Fax

Find Anyone Fast by Phone, Fax, Mail and Computer

The author, Richard S. Johnson, a nationally renowned expert on locating missing people, has brought together state-of-the-art methods necessary to find anyone quickly. This informative book describes hundreds of proven search techniques. It lists resources and assistance available from federal, state and local government agencies as well as business and private sources. Computer searches available to the public are described in detail.

The valuable information contained in this book includes:

- How to organize your search.
- How to gather information to begin your search.
- How to find important identifying information.
- How to use the information you obtain.
- How to obtain assistance from federal, state and local government agencies.
- How to determine if the person is deceased.
- Important laws that may affect your search.
- Computer searches available to you.
- Actual case studies so you can see how other searches have been successful.

"The best and most organized book I have ever owned on locating missing people." —*Jim Kroes, Private investigator & former federal investigator*

"...useful and insightful..."
—*PI Magazine*

Secrets of Finding Unclaimed Money

Richard Johnson again shows us how to search, but this time for unclaimed money. His expertise in locating people has brought him into a new field, heir searching.

Billions of dollars are in state unclaimed property offices, private companies, and life insurance proceeds just waiting for the rightful owner to come forward. However, many people are not aware of these funds or how easy it is to search and claim their money.

Billions of unclaimed dollars are in:

- Bank accounts
- Life insurance proceeds
- Retirement Funds
- Stocks and bonds
- Dividend checks
- Security deposits
- Trust funds
- Tax refunds
- Savings bonds
- Employment checks

Now discover how to:

- Find out if you or your family is due any unclaimed money from estates, the government or businesses.
- Make money by locating the rightful owners to estate and other unclaimed money.

Lists of all the resources you'll need:

- The unclaimed Property offices in all 50 states.
- Federal agencies holding unclaimed money.
- Financial organizations with unclaimed money.

Richard Johnson, the author, is a professional heir searcher who has helped hundreds of people claim money they never knew existed.

—Bookstore—

How to Investigate by Computer, Book II by Ralph D. Thomas. A manual of the new investigative technology that gives sources and teaches to investigate by computer. Learn about hard-to-find sources of information and how to access them. 130 pages, $34.95.

The Sourcebook of Federal Courts, US District and Bankruptcy. The definitive guide to searching for case information at the local level within the federal court system. Provides complete information on how to obtain criminal and civil court records and bankruptcy files from federal courts. 420 pages, $36.

The Sourcebook of County Court Records. A national guide of over 5,600 repositories of courthouse records. Provides information for obtaining copies of criminal, civil and probate court records. 1996 edition, 556 pages, $33.

The Sourcebook of County/Asset/Lien Records. A national guide to all county and city government agencies where real estate transactions, USS financing statements, and federal/state tax liens are recorded. 464 pages, $29.

The MVR Book: Motor Services Guide. A national reference detailing and summarizing, in practical terms, the description, access procedures, regulations and privacy restrictions of driver and vehicle records in all states. Check this book before attempting to locate people through state driver license and MVR offices. 272 pages, $18.

The Sourcebook of State Public Records. This book explains how to obtain information at the state level for business records, liens and security interest records, criminal records, worker's compensation, vital records, MVR, occupational licensing, business names, and permits. 360 pages, $33.

Order Form

MIE PUBLISHING
PO Box 17118
Spartanburg, SC 29301
(800) 937-2133

Publication	Price	Qty	Amount
Find Anyone Fast	$14.95		
How To Locate...Military	19.95		
Other books:			

Subtotal: $_____

South Carolina orders please add 5% sales tax _____

Postage and handling for first book 4.05

Please add $1.00 for each additional book. _____

(Please call for Int'l mail prices)

Total amount enclosed: $_____

_____

Visa, MasterCard, American Express Card   Expiration Date

_____

Name (Printed) and Signature

_____

Address   (Apt No.)

_____

City   State   Zip

(___) _____

Telephone Number

We accept government purchase orders!
All books are mailed Priority Mail.
Please remit this entire order form.

GLOSSARY

Armed Forces. Air Force, Army, Coast Guard, Marine Corps and Navy.

Base or Post Locator. An office or organization that has names and units of assignment of all military personnel assigned to a particular military installation, post or base.

Department of Veterans Affairs. Formerly called Veterans Administration. The abbreviation VA is used in this book.

Freedom of Information Act. Federal law requiring U.S. government agencies and the armed forces to release records to the public on request unless information is exempted by the Privacy Act or for national security reasons. Abbreviated FOIA.

Identifying Information. Information used to identify and locate someone such as name, SSN, service number, date of birth, ship, unit, etc.

National Archives. The federal depositories of historical documents. The National Personnel Records Center is part of the Archives.

Merchant Marines. The civilian maritime fleet.

Privacy Act. Federal law designed to protect an individual's constitutional right to privacy. The law also provides disclosure to an individual of information that the federal government maintains on that individual.

Rank. The grade or rating an individual holds in a military organization.

Reserve Components. Include the Air Force, Army, Coast Guard, Marine Corps and Navy reserve, and the Army National Guard and Air National Guard.

Retired Military Member. A person who has completed twenty or more years of duty in any of the military components and is receiving retired pay. He may be retired from an active or reserve component of a service (a member of a Reserve Component is not eligible for retired pay until age 60). A military member may be retired from active duty for disability due to injury or illness with less than 20 years of active service.

Service Number (SN). A number formerly used by the armed forces to identify individual members. The Army and Air Force discontinued using service numbers on July 1, 1969, the Navy and Marine Corps on July 1, 1972 and the Coast Guard on October 1, 1974. The Social Security number is now used in place of the service number.

Social Security Number (SSN). The nine digit number issued by the Social Security Administration and used by the uniformed services to identify individual members.

The Uniformed Services. The armed forces, the Public Health Service, and the National Oceanic and Atmospheric Administration.

Veteran. A person who has served on active duty in one or more of the armed forces. Individuals who have served only in the reserves or National Guard are not considered veterans.

World-Wide Locator. An office or organization operated by each of the uniformed services which maintains records containing the name, rank, SSN, date of birth, unit assignment and location of members of their respective service. World Wide Locators are operated for members on active duty, members of the reserves, and individuals who are retired.

INDEX

—Notes—